A NORTHERN CHILDHOOD

John Cooper

Grosvenor House
Publishing Limited

This book is published by
Grosvenor House Publishing Ltd
Link House
140 The Broadway, Tolworth, Surrey, KT6 7HT.
www.grosvenorhousepublishing.co.uk

A CIP record for this book
is available from the British Library

ISBN 978-1-83975-745-7

DEDICATIONS

To my mam, Gladys, who always wanted me to work in an office and not 'get my hands dirty'.

To my wife, Barbara, who put up with me while writing this book over several, sometimes barren, years.

To 'Slim John Cooper' from Nowell Road, who sadly died in New Zealand in 2019.

To my uncle Billy who introduced me to the joys and sorrows of watching Oldham Athletic

PREFACE

I suppose the question is: why did I write this book? The simplest way to answer this question is to go back to the 1960s, and an article in the now-defunct *News of the World* by Leo Abse, who was a Labour Party politician at the time. His simple message was that "everyone has a book in them", something which I have remembered all my life and have heard countless references to over the years from many different sources.

I started writing this book when I retired in 2010, a long time in the writing, and during this period I have enjoyed some very productive periods of putting pen to paper, as opposed to the fallow times when barely a word was written. I remember when at one of my several retirement parties during 2010 I was asked what I was going to do in my retirement. I boldly said, "Write a book about my early childhood in post-war North of England during the 1950s and early 1960s." I noticed one or two quizzical looks from my colleagues, who maybe thought I had had too much to drink and that the idea would soon be forgotten. One person who did not forget was Paul Louie, and in 2017, at a company reunion in Brussels, he asked me if the book had been completed. I did promise to send him a copy when completed, which I will certainly endeavour to do.

Another question is: why did I choose the first 16 years of my life? Despite the many hardships in post-war Britain, I was drawn to the misty nostalgia of this 'black and white' period, evoking memories of a simpler life. When writing this book, I promised myself that it would be done through my own eyes as I recollected what happened in my early life, and not necessarily via anecdotal stories from family members. However, I have to admit that I have included a number of stories provided by my sisters from when I was too young to remember.

As you read this book, my love of football runs through it like a stick of Blackpool rock. My recollections and memories of football have been many and varied, and were an important influence on my early life. My lifelong support of Oldham Athletic has been steadfast, and I have endured the many thick and thins (mainly thins) during the past 60-odd years. A proud moment for Oldham Athletic was when in 1992 they were one of the founding members of the football league. Hopefully, I do not sound too pompous by saying that football has been an important part of the social history of the UK since the second half of the 19th century, and I believe it has enriched many people's lives; it certainly has mine. In my final read-through of this book, the news broke of the plan for a European Super League for the so-called elite football clubs, something which would have been a complete anathema to me. Thankfully, the idiots left 'the room', and the sacrifice of the beautiful game on the altar of greed and avarice was defeated.

If I have offended anyone who is mentioned in this book, I offer my apologies in advance, as all my recollections have been honest and truthful.

PART ONE

THE BEGINNING

August was always the best month, being part of the long, seemingly endless summer holidays, but this was my last; my childhood was over. As I stood at the bus stop, waiting with the aroma-laden ladies from the local Pandora pickle factory, for the Number 17 bus to take me home after my last football game against the Slattocks village team, I realised my life was about to change forever. A job at the CWS (Cooperative Wholesale Society) beckoned. It was August 1964.

I was born on 21 April 1948 in Middleton, a Lancashire town sandwiched between Oldham and Rochdale and a few miles from Manchester. It was a good year if you were a Manchester United fan, as they won the FA Cup, defeating Blackpool 4–2 at Wembley in an exciting game. Stan Matthews would have to wait another five years for his famous Winners Medal. Many years later an ex-colleague from my days at ICI (Imperial Chemical Industries) told me the story of how he obtained tickets for the 1948 final. He and his father were returning from the semi-final by train, and by accident were sat near the match referee. He mentioned to the referee that he would like to go to the final in May but would not be able to obtain a ticket, at which point the referee asked for his address. He thought nothing about it until a few weeks before the final, when much to his surprise he received two tickets.

Then again, maybe 1948 was not a good year. Three years after the end of World War Two saw Britain bankrupt, suffering from post-war austerity and continued rationing, which would not end for several more years.

Middleton was a cotton town, as were all the other surrounding towns. The cotton industry was by 1948 in terminal decline, but the large mills still dominated the skyline, with their chimneys belching out their thick black smoke. The nearby town of Oldham was by 1900 the largest producer of spun cotton in the world, with 250 mills providing work for many thousands of people. Middleton was first and foremost a Lancashire town, despite its proximity to the large city of Manchester, and did not want to be associated with the 'Mancunians', as being a 'Lancastrian' was infinitely more important. I grew up in the town during the 1950s and 1960s, and despite the obvious grimness of that period, I still have fond memories of those years. Although I have very little recollection of my very early years, names of places are still etched in my mind for all kinds of reasons: Marsh Row, Little Park, Leater Street, Jackie Booth's field, The George pub and the 'Pee Gardens'.

My first two years were spent living at 2 Marsh Row, and I suppose the name maybe tells you everything you need to know about the dreadful housing conditions that people still had to endure in the UK halfway through the 20th century. Marsh Row was typical of the row upon row of streets, with dark and dingy back-to-back houses in the heartland of industrial Britain. These houses had very basic amenities, with tin baths in the kitchen and toilets in the backyard; toilet rolls were a luxury, so neatly cut newspapers squares hung on a nail on the wall.

Recollections of this time at Marsh Row were provided by my eldest sister, Glenys, who recounted the story of my father, mother, two sisters and baby John having to sleep in one bedroom, as the floorboards in the second bedroom were rotten, and thereby unsafe to be used. She also told the story of my mother and father one Xmas Day being drunk in bed after a heavy night of drinking at The George pub; wonder who looked after three young children! Another story, related to myself and Auntie Ethel (my father's feisty sister), was that she apparently stormed into our house in Marsh Row to tell my mother that there must be something seriously wrong with me, as she had observed me talking to myself in the street!

Living in this area of Middleton was very difficult and at times dangerous, and claimed the life of my father's mother, who after a heavy night of drinking at The George pub fell into the local canal and drowned.

In 1950 the Cooper family moved to a brand-new council estate which was a mile or so outside of the town centre. Hollin Estate was one of the thousands that were built by the Labour government after World War Two to replace the damaged houses and the dreadful housing which was to be found in the centre of most industrial towns in the UK.

The joys of a new semi-detached house at 47 Pershore Road were abundant. Gardens to the back and front of the house, living room, kitchen, three bedrooms, inside toilet with a bathroom, coalhouse, outside toilet and brick shed. We were definitely lucky people. The estate had wide roads, with very few cars in those early days, and plenty of green open spaces for children to play, the new houses being a far cry from what working-class people had been used to.

Sometimes socialism does work, the foundation of the National Health Service in 1946 being a shining example. We lived in what was the first phase of the estate, with Pershore Road, where we lived at Number 47, connecting to Nowell Road and Sherbourne Road. Furness Road ran the width of the estate, from Hollin Lane (the main Middleton to Heywood road) to Whalley Road, which was the extremity of the houses on the estate at the time.

Immediately behind our house was Hollins Green, around which were old people's bungalows where my mother worked as a home help in her later years and referred to the women she visited as 'my old ladies'. At the junction of Whalley Road and Nowell Road there was a roundabout with several handily placed local shops. There was a baker's, a butcher's, a hardware shop, a florist and a newsagent's run by the Williams family. These shops provided a vibrant hub for the people of the estate in an era when not many people had cars and shopping was a daily routine. In later years the estate expanded to at least twice its original size, swallowing up huge swathes of farmland, including my Auntie Ethel's farm (more of that story later), and eventually reaching Hollin Secondary School when it was built in the late 1950s.

I was one of four children: a brother, Donald, and sisters, Marlene and Glenys. None of us had middle names; I have told my grandchildren that we could not afford the cost of middle names!

Donald was 13 years older than me, being my half-brother, and was the result of an unfortunate relationship between my mother and a man who I know very little about, even to this day. I think the stigma of being born illegitimately in the 1930s stayed with him for the rest of his life, as it did, to a certain extent, with the rest of the family, particularly my mother. His life was blighted by a catastrophic marriage to a somewhat inappropriately named Gladys Jolly, who had serious mental health problems, and trying to bring up three young children in a such sad circumstances was very difficult, with their own lives to this day having been adversely affected. With hindsight, I personally feel a certain amount of guilt, in that maybe more could have been done to help Donald, particularly as he grew older and his health deteriorated.

When he died in September 2009, I uncovered a side to him that I did not know about. The old saying that 'you never really know someone' was never more true, and having told only a few family members of what I discovered, I will not say any more on this subject.

My mother was, in her own way, very protective of her first child. Although never discussed as a family, the guilt of bearing an illegitimate child was something that stayed with her, to some extent, for the rest of her life. To the eternal credit of my mother's parents, they accepted Donald into their family, and he lived with my mother at the family home on Stanley Road until she married in 1944.

I remember with some shame that when I was quite young, I stole some money from my brother; we slept in the same bedroom, and I took the money from his trouser pocket. I was questioned about the theft by my mother, but protested my innocence, and needless to say, I did not do anything like that ever again.

Glenys is four years older than me, and while I was growing up, although she was very much around, the relatively large age gap meant that she did not figure much in my life at that time, unlike my other sister, Marlene, who was closer in age. I suppose Glenys was my 'big' sister. She married relatively young and eventually had three children. She and her husband, John, ran the local post office and newsagent's for many years in Shaw, near Oldham. Sadly, John died in his early fifties from leukaemia.

While writing this book, she recounted a story about my father, who was a man of few words, but when he 'put his foot down', that was it. Not sure how old she was, maybe not long after leaving school, she wanted to become a nanny, which would have meant living away from home. My father was adamant that she was not allowed to accept the job, and there was no further discussion. This type of attitude from parents in the 1950s and 1960s was very common, and the lives of young people were sometimes impacted by these somewhat misguided decisions. My wife, Barbara, wanted to be a nurse, but her parents would not allow her to follow this profession, as it was not considered to be a 'proper' job.

Marlene is only two years older than me, and I was close to her, not least because we both attended the same schools at both primary and secondary level. Marlene was, and still is, a free-spirited and independent lady, and is today very much living the good life with her second husband in the delightful Dordogne area of South West France. Our father was in the main an even-tempered person, but when he got his 'hair off', he was a force to be reckoned with, and Marlene once tested him to the limit. My sister was a talented singer, and my mother managed to scrape the money together so she could have lessons to improve her voice. The lessons were with Jimmy Hyde, who among other things was a talented local cricketer and for many years played for Middleton in the Central Lancashire League. Such was the quality of my sister's voice that somehow (not sure how it happened) she was offered the opportunity to go and sing in Germany at the many US military bases. This was discussed at home, and my father was adamant that she was not going to sing in Germany. I suppose, in fairness to him, he was probably trying to protect her from what he saw as a potentially dangerous situation for such a young girl of 18 years old. Marlene would not give up, and continued to plead to be allowed to go, targeting our mother, and eventually the whole situation boiled over. It was late one evening, and my father was upstairs preparing to go bed. Marlene was downstairs with my mother, who was getting more and more upset by this matter. My sister then went to her room, and my mother went upstairs to go to bed and continue the discussion with my father. All of a sudden, I heard my father shouting and swearing, and he came out of the bedroom to confront my sister. By the way, never underestimate the speed at which a man with a wooden leg can move. Marlene, realising she was in big trouble, quickly opened the window in her bedroom and jumped onto the flat roof of the brick shed before climbing down onto the path running up the side of the house. From there, she ran to a friend's house, whose mother ran the local children's orphanage. A little later my mother came into my room and asked me to go and fetch Marlene, as it was safe to come home because my father had taken his leg off and was now in bed—a little black humour in what had been a volatile night. Marlene did not go to Germany.

Our dad, John, was in his own way a complex man, who, if I am honest with myself, I did not know very well. His early life must have been very difficult, born in 1917 during World War One in the tough environment of the northern industrial town that was Middleton. His father does not appear to have been a good father, and the story of his typical Xmas as a young boy probably tells us all we need to know about him. Xmas in those days was not a time of great happiness; the struggle to survive was still ever present. On the eve of Xmas, my father first had to chop firewood, bundle it up and then sit outside the local pub selling it, and he was not allowed to come home until everything had been sold. On Xmas day, the old adage of an apple, an orange and some seasonal nuts, with just maybe a small present, was what he received.

My father, for the majority of his adult life, bore the tragedy of only having one leg, which must have scarred him both emotionally and physically. Kenneth Allsop, a well-known BBC presenter in the 1960s and 1970s, also had one leg, and recounted not only the physical pain from the nerve ends of his stump, particularly during damp and cold weather, but also the psychological stress and strain of living with the loss of a leg. The circumstances surrounding the loss of his leg were never discussed within the family, and my mother, even after my father died, never mentioned what had happened to him. All the papers relating to his accident were, for many years, in a tin box at the bottom of my parents' wardrobe, and one Xmas, when I was rooting around for my presents, I had the opportunity to read them. During the 1930s, the economic depression left many people without jobs, and it was only during the years leading up to World War Two that government projects provided people with work. My father worked on a road gang, building new roads in the south-east of England, and after a night of hard drinking with his workmates, he was hit by a bus as they made their way back to their lodgings along an unlit road, subsequently losing his right leg. He was unable to obtain any compensation from the bus company, as they claimed that he was drunk and, therefore, significantly contributed to the accident. The contents of the tin box subsequently disappeared, almost certainly destroyed by my mother. A pity, as I would have liked to have studied them more carefully as I became older.

Further information came to light in what you might call an anecdote to this story on the eve of my wedding to my wife, Barbara, in 1977, not long before my Auntie Ethel died. Auntie Ethel was a larger-than-life character who said it how it was, and her description upon seeing her brother after his accident, in what she described as blood-spattered walls in a hospital ward, left very little to the imagination. While writing this book, I came across an envelope, which I assume had contained a letter, addressed to Mr J. Cooper, B2 Ward, c/o County Hospital, Redhill, Surrey, circa 1938—the last surviving evidence of that terrible time for my father.

Despite his disability, he always managed to work in a variety of jobs, although he did suffer periods of unemployment, which meant that I had to suffer his cooking. His last job was with Verson Engineering Company, where he managed their stockroom, and by all accounts, he did an excellent job. When he returned from work each day, my mother would have a pint pot of hot tea ready for him, and this would last him all evening; he really must have like cold tea! My father's sudden death in 1977, at what is the now the ridiculously young age of 60, was a deep shock at the time, but with hindsight, he was an old man, after years of smoking and drinking, in addition to having only one leg for more than half his life. On his death, I helped my mother to sort out his papers (not many) and came across a tax form which he had been endeavouring to complete. One of the questions was, "Do you have any money in a bank or building society?", to which he said, "Don't know." Not sure what the tax man would have thought about that reply, since he actually had several thousand pounds in the bank.

Our mam, Gladys, was the rock of our family, stoically putting up with whatever life threw at her, and in her own inimitable way was fiercely protective of her four children. Her own family, albeit very much working class, was a cut above the 'common herd', in that her father, Henry, was a member of the engineering team at the local cotton mill, his job being to keep the mill operating almost 365 days a year. This was an important job, bringing with it a certain standing in the local community. Therefore, it was with some shame and horror when their unmarried daughter, Gladys, became pregnant at the age of 21; the father of the unborn child, Donald, not being someone she was likely to marry. The shame of an unmarried mother in the 1930s is difficult to imagine, particularly when measured against today's moral standards, but to her parents eternal credit, they decided to bring the child up in their own family, my mother having two younger brothers who so to speak took Donald 'under their wing'.

Her marriage to my father in June 1943 was possibly what you might call 'a marriage of convenience', in that you had two people who brought to the marriage a certain amount of baggage. Between 1943 and 1948 she had three children; maybe my father, despite his one leg, was trying to prove that he was 'a real man'. The relationship between my father and mother was sometimes a difficult one, with, as they both got older, tolerance and affection replacing what was initially love. When my mother was much older, and after my father's death, she casually informed my younger sister, Marlene, that my father had not kissed or touched her from the day I was born. She probably was a woman who needed some kind of physical contact in her life, not necessarily sexual, and this need came out in several quite unusual ways. I remember when she was going to see Dr Rose, the family GP, possibly something about 'women's problems', and she always wore clean underwear. I am sure nothing improper happened during such visits, but it was a form of physical contact with a man.

Such were the family finances that my mother had to work to make ends meet, and when I went to school, she worked in the clothing trade at Harry Bell's factory in Middleton for many years. This was hard physical work making military uniforms, tents, etc., the fashion industry being some years away. Working five days a week with a young, growing family in the 1950s was not easy; the days of husbands doing their bit to help were a long way in the future, and my mother just had to 'get on with it'. The highlight of my mother's week was going to the Dyers and Polishers Club on Saturday and Sunday evenings, and she loved to get up and sing. My father died when only 60 years old, so my mother was a widow almost half her life, which I would like to think were initially happy years in her little flat on Torre Close, before the onset of dementia forced her into a residential home for the final years of her life. My own children affectionately nicknamed her 'Glad Arse, The

Happy Bum', as she spent many patience-filled years playing with them.

The wider Cooper family (my father and mother both had the same surname) were a somewhat rum bunch, particularly on my father's side.

Auntie Ethel was of a similar age to my father, but of an entirely different temperament. Ethel was a feisty lady who always called a spade a spade, and certainly was the boss at home; her husband, Jimmy, was a gentle soul, and definitely did as he was told. She had two children, Jimmy and Gerald, myself being much closer in age to Gerald. I remember once when Gerald had an accident on his bike. He rode into the back of a parked car while riding up Hollin Lane! He dared not go home, as he would have got little sympathy from his mother, so he came to our house to see his Auntie Gladys, who patched him up before sending him home.

Ethel and her other siblings were always falling out over relatively trivial things, and these situations could last for long periods of time. She did like a drink, and when my father died in December 1977, she, along with her younger sister, Stella, came to our house (I had married my wife Barbara in the October of that year) to console my mother. Between them they drank a bottle of whisky, and Ethel's son, Jimmy, had to come and take them home, as they were both well and truly pissed.

Auntie Stella was several years younger than my father, and was a glamorous woman, with immaculate hair and make-up, and in later years she acquired a Spanish suntan. Her husband, Alan, was a local policeman in the Moston area of Manchester, and his daily beat patrol took him around some of the toughest areas of the district in the 1950s and 1960s. He lived in the Moston area and got to know most of the local criminals. As he got older, they tended, at his request, to conduct their criminal activities (mostly petty crimes) away from his patrol route, as he was only several years from retirement. In fact, he left the police force early, thereby missing out on a good pension; something which I suspect he regretted in later life. Stella always wanted something better, and if I remember rightly, she wanted to move to Blackpool to open a boarding house or a small hotel, which they did; but it did not work out, and Alan ended up working in various low-paid jobs for the rest of his working life. In later life, Stella enjoyed many holidays in Spain with her friends, escaping the drab weather of Manchester.

Auntie Gladys was the person I knew least, and along with Uncle Billy was much younger than my Dad, Ethel and Stella. In fact, Gladys and Billy did not spend much time with their parents, and from an early age they were brought up by family friends. My only real memory of Auntie Gladys was when she and her family emigrated to Australia and my mother and I visited them just before they left, their house being full of boxes containing their possessions. My elder sister, Glenys, disputes this story, partly because they were 'Twenty Pound Poms' flying to Australia, rather than going by sea as 'Ten Pound Poms', and luggage was restricted, so maybe I was mistaken. In 2011 my wife and I visited my Auntie Gladys in Adelaide, where she and her family had settled since emigrating, and I met my cousins, Peter and Lynn. Sadly, Bob, her husband, was suffering from dementia and only just about realised who we were.

Uncle Billy was the uncle I knew best of all, due to our shared love of Oldham Athletic. Not the brightest pebble on the beach, but a man with a heart of gold, as you will see later in the book. As with Gladys, he was brought up by family friends, my grandmother having died and I assume my grandfather being unable to look after Gladys and him. He was a typical working man, and enjoyed a drink, a cigarette and a bet. When he died in the late 1990s, I did not attend his funeral, as I was living abroad at the time—something which I now regret.

My mother's side of the family were not such a rum bunch, as she had three brothers, Fred, Kenneth and Ernest.

Uncle Fred was the eldest of the four children, my mother being closer in age to him than Kenneth and Ernest. There was a definite love-hate relationship between my mother and Fred, typified to some extent by the greeting she gave him when after many years he turned up out of the blue at my grandmother's house. "Bloody hell! Look what the cat has dragged in."

Fred had a highly strung wife, who I never met, and my mother would always refer to her as Jenny Burke, her maiden name. He lived in Blackpool for many years, so was rarely seen at Stanley Road, my grandparents' home, but as is always the case, he was the favourite son.

Uncle Kenneth was, I think, of the three brothers, the one closest to my mother, and very supportive of her, particularly in the years when Donald was being brought up by my grandparents and the stigma of illegitimacy was alive and kicking. I know he took Donald to watch Oldham Athletic on a regular basis, and he told me the story/joke about waiting outside the ground one Saturday when the game had already kicked off and suddenly there was an almighty roar. He asked the person nearest to him, "Have Latics scored?", the reply being, "No, the meat pies have arrived."

He was married to Auntie Jean, who is still alive today, and they had a son, my cousin, David, who was a similar age to me, spending part of our summer holidays together at each other's houses. He was always a cheerful person who took great pleasure in pulling my leg about the addresses my wife and I lived at in The Netherlands and Belgium, which to him were unpronounceable.

Uncle Ernest was the youngest of the four children, and without a doubt the most laid back. He was married to Auntie Ivy, and to quote the terminology of the time 'she was never a well woman', which put an extra burden on him with regards to their two children, Bernard and Nicholas. For several years my sister Marlene would accompany them on holiday, providing an extra pair of hands. She was particularly good with Bernard when he was very young.

Initially, they lived near the centre of Rochdale, quite close to the place where the famous singer/actress, Gracie

Fields, was born. Ernest definitely liked a drink, and it was more than the odd one or two pints; maybe he was escaping his increasingly difficult family life. One of his pubs was the Cemetery Inn, which was next to the local cemetery in Rochdale. The story told by him was that on leaving the pub one night, somewhat the worse for wear, he was walking down the road when he saw a man wearing a Guy Fawkes style hat walk casually through the wall surrounding the cemetery and off up the road. He quickly made his way home to tell his wife, Ivy, of this crazy story, which she put down to drinking too much beer. He was an incredibly hard-working man, and for many years after Ivy's death he worked the night shift at a factory in Stockport, almost until the day he died.

47 Pershore Road

This is where we moved to in 1950, being part of a post-war council housing estate, and after 70 years I can still remember the names of the people who lived on the road. They were a bit like football teams in the 1950s and 1960s, when the names never changed, in that players never moved to other clubs, as they were all paid the maximum wage of £20, regardless of which team they played for. The people who lived on Pershore Road in the 1950s also did not move, as there was nowhere else to go, due to the lack of private housing. This was our side of the road:

The Burtons (our next-door neighbours) – Doris, Billy, Susan and the Graysons.

Doris was a small feisty woman with, what I recall, tremendous energy and determination; and I vividly recall when she was well into her seventies how she tackled what was a large garden and rescued it from the 'weeds'. Billy, Doris's husband, was a kind man, with a shock of black hair, who I did not know very well, and he died relatively young of TB. There is a great photo of Billy with Susan and me sat on the doorstep. Susan was the girl next door, a bit younger than me, and for many years I thought she was Doris's daughter, despite Doris's age, whereas in fact she was the illegitimate daughter of Jean, the somewhat wayward daughter of Doris and Billy.

The Graysons – Thomas and Sarah had run the George Pub on Manchester New Road in Middleton from 1927 to 1954 and upon retirement had gone to live with Doris at Pershore Road. My memories of Tom Grayson, who my Dad knew well from his frequenting of the George, were of his love of gardening, which must have come as a welcome relief from all those years behind the bar of a smoky old pub. He turned the Burton's back garden into a mini market garden, growing all sorts of vegetables and fruit, my favourite being his wonderful strawberries, which my dad also started to grow after Tom had given him some plants. I cannot remember when he died, as it appeared that one minute he was there in the garden, and then he was not. I did not think too much about it. Mrs Grayson, never thought of her as Sarah, was someone who I associated with looking after Susan while Doris worked, and she made the most wonderful brown chips, cooked in traditional lard, which Susan used to eat sat on the back doorstep, with me looking on longingly. Still cannot remember if Susan ever let me eat any of those chips.

The Shoremans (our other next-door neighbours) – Fred, Mrs Shoreman, Beverley, Neil and Ian.

I suppose Fred was a man of some substance, being a manager at a local engineering firm, and at times he and my mother had several confrontations, mainly over 'the kids', my mother always giving as good as she got. My memory of Mrs Shoreman was of an excitable woman who I suspect at times wound Fred up over something and nothing. Beverley was the eldest of the children, a few years younger than me, and went onto the local grammar school, a rare occurrence on Pershore Road. Neil and Ian were several years younger than me, but were some of my 'football buddies'; Ian in particular at a very young age being a feisty competitor.

The Middlehursts – Harry, Edna, Geoffrey and his sister, Gwen.

Harry Middlehurst was, in my young memory, a big, powerful man, who was one of the few people to own a car on our road in the post-war austerity era of the 1950s. The car I particularly remember was a red sports car, which we all went to Southport in one Sunday; and to this day, I am not sure how we all managed to fit into such a small car. Harry was always tinkering with his cars, as well as those belonging to other people, and the scene outside his house was sometimes reminiscent of a car garage. There was always something about Harry which I could not quite understand, and with the benefit of hindsight, I suppose it was that 'he fancied himself' with the ladies; nothing specific, but in later years I did hear that he had left his wife for a younger woman who worked with him at the local swimming baths.

Edna, Harry's wife, was a quiet, almost anonymous, person who I suppose had a lot to put up with. Geoffrey was the same age as me, so we knew each other very well, going to the same school and playing football and cricket together; although at times he could be a divisive person in the life of the children on the road.

The Ewarts – Denis, Gertie, Christine, Carol(?), David and Stephen(?).

Denis Ewart did not work in what you might call a proper job, in that he played in a band during the evening, so he was always around during the day, which I never quite understood, as all the other men were at work. A memory of Denis was that he always ate his meals on a tray while sat in his chair in front of the television, something I thought at the time was strange, as we always ate our meals at the kitchen table.

Gertie was, I suspect, not a well woman. The strain of bringing up four children plus a 'relaxed' husband eventually took its toll, and heart problems followed. Christine and Carol were more my age, and as they did not play football, I was not much interested in them. Their brothers were much more fertile territory for our Pershore Road football team.

The Jowetts – Mrs and Mrs Jowett, Paul and his sisters.

The Jowetts were somewhat apart from the rest of us, in that in another era they would not have been living in a council house. Their house and garden were always immaculate, and there was always the impression that they were a hard-working family. Paul was a few years older than me, and a person who was always making things, their brick shed having been turned into a very impressive workshop. There were two sisters, Joyce and Eileen, who were several years older than me, one of whom when married emigrated to Canada.

The Matthews – Charlie, Jessie, Billy and Sheila.

Charlie and Jessie were older than the other parents in the road, but, nevertheless, were lovely people, and when I saw them, they always appeared to be in a hurry going somewhere. Billy was much older than me, as was Sheila, who was a good friend of my two sisters.

The Hiltons – Mr and Mrs Hilton, Mick, John and sister.

I did not really know much about Mr and Mrs Hilton, but was friendly with Mick and John. Mick saw himself as a bit of a hard nut, but was more of an angry young man.

John was a bit younger than me, and once again an occasional player in the Pershore Road football team.

The Darlingtons – Jack, wife, John and Gillian.

Jack was a small local builder, probably a lot wealthier than the rest of the people living on Pershore Road, and eventually moved to a house overlooking the Middleton Cricket Club, which cost him the princely sum of £3,000 in the early 1970s. By the early 1980s it was worth

10 times the original price, and today would be worth about £200,000. This was the house that my mother and father considered buying at the time, but in the end they were afraid of making what for them would have been a monumental decision. The mentality of living in a council house was something my parents could not let go of, as was typical of their generation. John, the son, who was much older than me, was an excellent footballer and eventually emigrated to Australia. Gillian, the daughter, was younger than me and probably came as a surprise to the family at the time of her birth. She was a very pretty young girl, and over the years turned into a beautiful woman. She was definitely somewhat spoiled by her parents, exemplified by her driving around the area in her Mini Cooper. Wonder what happened to her.

The Berrys - Joe, Enid, Barbara, Sylvia and John.

Joe Berry, a true northern, working-class man if ever there was one, enjoyed a drink, and maybe a bet, and always appeared to be a happy-go-lucky sort of a person. Many years later I met his daughter, Sylvia, at the funeral of Susan Burton, and she told me the story of how Joe would ring the local taxi company and ask them to bring a bottle of whisky to his home. Amazingly, Joe's wife, Enid, is still alive today, living happily with her daughter, Sylvia. John was a similar age to me and was a bit of a lad, although not a great footballer, but a big Manchester United fan.

Now for the other side of the road:

The Phillips

This was the 'awkward brigade' family, it being in many ways a sad situation. The Phillips lived at the end of Pershore Road, and their garden was at the side of the house, facing onto two triangles of green grass, which was where all the kids played football. Inevitably, the ball ended up in their garden, and there was always trouble when we asked for it back.

There was Walter, his wife and his two children, David and his brother, who were never allowed to play with us—something which I think was quite cruel and possibly impacted their future lives. My mother and Walter had several run-ins, and one famous incident was on a Friday evening in 1962 while I was watching the World Cup football highlights in Chile. Walter, after consuming several pints of beer at the pub, knocked on our front door and proceeded to harangue my mother about what I had been doing earlier in the day outside his house. My mother's response was to say "Go home you silly bugger", and she pushed him away from the door, at which point he fell over the privets and ended up flat on his back on the lawn. He then staggered home, threatening all kinds of retribution.

The Buntings

Stan was originally from Canada and worked long hours in the printing industry. An affable man who appeared to be a somewhat happy-go-lucky-person; very much a contrast to the other men living on Pershore Road. His wife was a nice lady who stoically bore the brunt of bring up their two children, David and his brother.

The Hiltons

Mr and Mrs Hilton were the hard-working parents of David and Angela, and made sure their children had the best possible start in life, sending them both to a private school in Rochdale. They were one of the families who eventually moved to private housing once the post-war council-house building boom was over. David was part of the Pershore Road football team and was very lithe and quick, something which did not always please me, as I was relatively fat and slow. His sister, Angela, was a beautiful young girl, almost doll-like, with goldilocks-type hair, and although she was several years younger than me, I was always in awe of her. In later life she married Peter Collins, a famous speedway rider of the 1970s and 1980s.

The Penmans

I cannot remember much about Mr and Mrs Penman, only that they had one son, Alan, yet another member of the Pershore Road football team, who at times could be moody and would not always join in with the other kids in the road.

The Paynes

Alf and Winnie Payne lived near 'the steps' and had two sons, Stephen and Michael, the former being once again a member of our Pershore Road football team. Only as I grew older did I find out that Alf Payne had been a prisoner of war of the Japanese during World War Two, and continued to suffer from this experience for many years.

The Thompsons

Finally, the Thompsons, who were to some extent 'the outsiders', in that they had a son, Trevor, who as we used to say was 'not quite right'. He was a huge lad, at least twice as big as the rest of us, and was not allowed to play with the other kids because of his boisterous and potentially dangerous behaviour. His mother, who in a strange kind of way I always admired, bore the brunt of coping with Trevor. My most vivid recollections were of her struggling down the road with him and trying to keep control of him, as he was a powerful young boy. It was particularly difficult for Mrs Thompson when we were all playing football or cricket, as Trevor always wanted to join in, and I remember on one occasion when he managed to get hold of our football and bounce it high up into the air. We all stood there with our mouths wide open.

His father was a strange character, who always seemed to be working, and came across as somewhat sad. I suspect Trevor's parents were quite old when he was born, which maybe explained his condition, a burden that they had to carry on their own until I stopped seeing him with his mother. This must have been when he became too big and strong for his parents to cope with him, and I suppose he ended up in one of those out of sight out of mind mental institutions, which thankfully no longer exist.

The Family Home

The house on Pershore Road was the family home for almost 50 years, and in many respects did not change much during this period. Downstairs there was a living room, kitchen and pantry. In the living room was a grey three-piece suite, which we seemed to have had forever, and over the years the wear and tear became very evident and had to be hidden by strategically placed covers, courtesy of my mother's handiwork with the sewing machine. The carpet, which only covered part of the room, must have looked good when it was new, but I only ever remember it being somewhat threadbare, which caused me some embarrassment, as I did not want my friends to see how poor we were. Where there was no carpet, we had linoleum, good old lino, on which stood the family pride and joy: the walnut table and four chairs. I can count on the fingers of one hand the number of times it was used—something to be enjoyed on special occasions. One such occasion was on New Year's Eve, 1960, when Bert and Ada Lowe, family friends, came for their tea. Why I remember the exact date is because my beloved Oldham Athletic beat Southport 11–0 on a snow-covered Boundary Park pitch on a very cold day; hence the nickname 'Ice Station Zebra'. Many years later, when my mother decided to move to a flat nearby, the walnut table and chairs went with her, shoehorned into her tiny living room and never used again.

These new houses did not have central heating, and the only real source of heating was from a coke stove in the kitchen for heating the hot water and an open coal fire in the living room, both having to be prepared each morning for lighting.

The kitchen was, I suppose with hindsight, quite small, but seemed in my small eyes to be huge, with so many things crammed into the space, especially as the kitchen table expanded into a makeshift table-tennis table with limited elbow room. Attached to the kitchen ceiling was 'the rack', on which wet clothes were placed to dry in the heat from the coke stove.

The pantry was the coolest place in the house, where the perishable food was kept—this being in the days before affordable fridges and freezers were available to working-class people. The 'meat safe' was the modern-day equivalent of the fridge: a wooden cabinet with several shelves, and fine mesh at the front to keep the flies at bay. I suppose the meat safe was the start of my lifelong aversion to any form of do-it-yourself, in that my mother once asked me to paint it, and I proceeded to leave more of the blue paint on the floor than on the meat safe. Needless to say, she never asked me again.

There were four bedrooms: one for my parents, a bedroom each for my sisters, Marlene and Glenys, and the other bedroom for Donald and me. In addition, there was a toilet and bathroom—a far cry from the outside toilet and tin bath at Marsh Row.

Upstairs was by far the coldest part of the house, with no heating in any of the rooms, albeit for the small electric fire. Needless to say, on cold winter nights nobody lingered when undressing, particularly if the bed was being warmed by a hot-water bottle.

Outside at the front of the house there was a garden consisting of a lawn, privets and several bushes—something which my father took great pride in keeping neat and tidy, as did the majority of people on Pershore Road. A garden provided space and fresh air for people to enjoy, and our back garden was no exception, in that my father created a place with concrete paths and small walls which contained flower beds and fruit and vegetable growing areas. The lawn, with a wooden trellis to support the climbing roses, was the centrepiece of the garden for many years, particularly for those few short years when Tom Gracen looked after our garden as well as his own.

Attached to the rear of the house were the coalhouse, which housed our supply of coal and coke, another toilet—a two-toilet house (very posh)—and, finally, the brick shed, which served many purposes: workshop and storage of garden equipment, and it was also where I played 'doctors and nurses' with Avril Buckingham! It was also where the Co-op delivery man left our weekly grocery order; Tesco, and others, did not invent home delivery. Down the side of the house was a path, which on many occasions doubled as a place to play cricket—a poor man's version of a cricket net!

I cannot remember much of my early life at Pershore Road prior to going to school. I do remember being ill with the mumps and having to play in the back garden while I was contagious. These were happy days, playing for hours on end at the bottom of the garden with my motor cars and toy soldiers, creating roads in the soil and building houses from bits of wood and twigs. I also remember my father, who was temporarily unemployed at the time, taking me to see the start of the building of the houses on the Manchester overspill estate which became known as Langley.

During World War Two, Manchester suffered terrible damage as a result of German bombing, and many thousands of houses were completely destroyed or rendered unfit for habitation. When the war finished there was an urgent need for new housing, and Manchester looked beyond their own boundaries for places to build such houses, and throughout the 1950s and 1960s I saw the growth and development of both Langley and Hollin Estate, separated only by Hollin Lane. Eventually, Langley grew to 25,000 people, and doubled the size of the population of Middleton. Inevitably, this mass movement of people from the inner suburbs of Manchester caused certain friction with the 'Middletonians', and for many years my friends and I regarded it as 'Mau Mau' country, and you only ventured across Hollin Lane onto the Langley Estate at your peril.

Hollin Estate continued to grow in size, and by the late 1950s it was starting to encroach on neighbouring farmland, and this coincidentally impacted on the wider Cooper family. My Great Aunt Ethel and Great Uncle Archie owned a farm which was in the path of the housing development, and after receiving compensation from the local council, they left their home and retired to live in Higher Wycombe. I remember visiting the farmhouse a few days before it was demolished, and at this time it had already been vandalised and there were plenty of people around stripping whatever they could from the building. Strangely enough, I had never previously been to the farmhouse, even though we lived within a short distance, but I was glad that I went, as it must have been an impressive building in its prime. The bottom floor consisted of a large living/cooking area with two flights of stairs, one at each end of the room, leading to a landing which stretched the whole width of the room, with several doors leading to bedrooms and a bathroom. Within a few days there was nothing left.

PART TWO

PARKFIELD PRIMARY SCHOOL

Upon reaching five years old in 1953, the year of the famous Stanley Matthews FA Cup Final, I was old enough to go to school. It was decided that I would go to Parkfield Primary School, which was located in the centre of the town close to where we used to live in Marsh Row. There were plans to build a junior school on Hollin Estate, but not before I needed to go to school. The area of Parkfield was the 'old part' of Middleton, close to the town centre, with most of the housing in the immediate vicinity of the school being of the two-up-two-down terraced category. Parkfield was a Church of England school, with the church perched on a hill overlooking the school, situated in the posh area of Archer Park—the houses being a cut above the more modest houses surrounding the school.

Parkfield Primary School was opened on 28 June 1864 and catered for infants, aged 4 to 7 years old, and juniors, aged 8 to 11 years old. The infant section was on the lower level and consisted of a single-storey building with two classrooms separated by a flexible dividing wall which opened up into a large room for things like school assemblies and Xmas parties. A third classroom had large, almost floor-to-ceiling, windows, which provided a bright environment for the children to learn in. The playground was at the back of the classrooms, bordered on two sides by walls made of vertical stone slabs held in place by metal clamps. On the third side of the playground was the school hall, which was the place where the 'dreaded' school dinners were served. To get to the school hall you had to go down a sloping walkway of uneven stone slabs, complete with skylight. To the right of the walkway there were somewhat primitive toilets, not quite outside or inside, and further down was the kitchen where the school dinners were prepared for serving, after being brought in each day from somewhere in Middleton, where they had been cooked. There was always that air of expectation as we entered the school hall for our dinner, as the smell was tempting, although the reality of immediate post-war food proved to be somewhat different. The best part of the dinners were the puddings—semolina with a dollop of jam being my favourite. I only have good memories of my first years at school, the teachers being kind and considerate, particularly Mr and Mrs Howarth, who in my then small world seemed to have been there forever.

Xmas at Parkfield in the austere post-war days was a magical time, with the two classrooms made into one large room where we could play games and eat lots of jelly and cakes—a real treat for the pupils.

With me going to school, my mother could then resume her work in the clothing industry at Harry Bell's in

Middleton. Each day my sister Marlene and I would catch the Number 17 or the Number 63 bus to Middleton, and then make the short walk to Parkfield, usually stopping off at Poole's sweetshop to spend our penny. Mr and Mrs Poole, an elderly couple, ran the sweetshop for many years, and I will always remember their wonderful home-made ice lollies, even better, as they were only a halfpenny in old money.

From their shop, I would walk up the street to a set of what probably were in better days ornamental steps, and would then go past a small play area with swings and slides, and immediately behind this area was, for me, the famous 'red rec', where my football career started. From there I climbed another set of identical steps, and Parkfield School loomed on my left.

During my time at Parkfield, we endured some pretty bad winters with lots of snow and heavy rain. However, the pea-souper was by far the worst, it being an almost impenetrable, thick, acrid fog, which descended upon Middleton during the winter months. In the early 1950s coal was used by both industry and the people who still lived in the centre of the town, and this created a lot of pollution in the atmosphere. On such occasions it was quicker to walk home from school rather than use the bus, usually with Jack Ramsden's mother, the cliché being 'you could not see your hands in front of your face' being very apt.

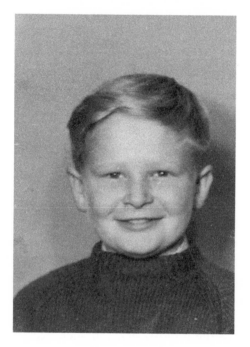

A good-looking lad.

Visiting Father Xmas with
my sisters, Marlene and Glenys.

Pershore Road football team.
A right motley crew!

We all longed for the day when we could leave the infant part of the school and join the 'big' boys and girls in the junior section, and this duly arrived after three years. The step up to the junior section initially took me outside of my cosy little world of the past three years, but my recollections are still as vivid today as they were then.

This part of the school consisted of three large classrooms down the centre of the building, once again separated by flexible partitions, thereby allowing for a large hall to be created for school gatherings.

At one end of the building there was a stage for what were limited musical or drama events, and at the other end of the building there were two smaller classes. The teachers were a mixture of the old and new, or you could say pre- and post-World War Two. The headmaster was Mr Griffiths, a seemingly stern and serious person of the 'old school', and for certain you did not want to be sent to his office for any misdemeanour, as the cane, either on the hand or the backside, was given out liberally. I suppose we all lived in fear of Mr Griffiths, and it was only several years later that my sister Marlene, who was then a hairdresser, started to do his wife's hair, and the nice and ordinary retired Mr Griffith emerged from his school persona.

My first teacher was Miss Burgess, a spinster who lived at Middleton Junction and was a staunch churchgoer, and I suspect spent the whole of her working life at Parkfield. She was of that breed of teachers who espoused discipline and distance from the children—her maxim, somewhat adulterated, being that the child should be seen but not always heard. I often wondered what happened to her after she retired, as school and church seemed to be the mainstays of her life.

My next teachers were very much younger and represented the future of the school as the 'old guards' gradually retired. Miss Dugdale was, in my small eyes, a very young teacher and always appeared to be cheerful, which came through in the way she taught the children in her class—very different from Miss Burgess, who I suppose, to be fair, 'knocked us into shape' during our first year at junior level. Miss Dugdale lived on Durnford Street, which was in walking distance of Parkfield, and I often saw her as I made my way home after school going into what I assumed was her parents' house. This act of normality made her appear human, in that she did have a life after school, whereas other teachers disappeared home to places I did not know, making them almost mythical in my childlike eyes.

Mrs Thornton was my next teacher, and in my innocent young eyes I was for a while in love with her and craved her attention; so much so that one day when I was feeling unwell, I lay down on the floor at the back of the classroom hoping she would notice me. After so many years it is hard to be absolutely sure, but if I remember correctly, I think she ignored me or maybe did not see me, so I got better very quickly. I believe she or her husband came from Canada, and eventually they returned to Canada, which always gave her that air of being different from the run-of-the-mill teachers at the school.

In my final year at Parkfield, my teacher was the formidable Mrs Taylor, or as my mother called her, Lizzie Saxon, this being her maiden name when she taught her in the 1920s. She was definitely 'old school', and was a teacher with a fearsome reputation who you did not ever cross for fear of eternal retribution. She was very much coming to the end of her teaching career in the late 1950s, and there was probably one incident which maybe told her it was time to go. As mentioned earlier, Middleton had seen the population of the town almost double since World War Two with the building of Langley Estate, and there was a massive influx of people from the bombed-out suburbs of Manchester. Manchester people were different from us Middletonians, and Lawrence Dale was definitely different from the rest of us! As there was a shortage of places at the schools on Langley, several children were sent to Parkfield, including Lawrence Dale. He was what you might call a lippy boy, with his respect for authority being borderline—a very different person from the rest of us, who were more subservient. We were 'townies', and he was from the big city. On the particular day of the incident, Mrs Taylor was on playground duty, and when it was time for us to go back to our classrooms, we all lined up by class ready to go inside. There was always someone who did not get into line fast enough, and a simple "hurry up" was usually sufficient; but not on this day, as it was Lawrence Dale who was messing around. Mrs Taylor, in her sergeant-major voice, told him to get into line, to which he calmly replied, "Fuck off." There are moments in your life when time appears to stand still and everything goes very quiet; this was one such moment. I, and many of the other children, could not believe what we had heard. Indeed, for me it was probably the first time I'd heard these words said in such a public manner at the school. Mrs Taylor was momentarily stunned, but recovered her somewhat shaky composure to send him immediately to Mr Griffiths, and a caning of biblical proportions was no doubt administered.

Mrs Taylor lived not far from the local cricket club, and when she retired in the early 1960s, I would see her with her friends at the match on a Saturday afternoon. She appeared almost human outside of the constraints of her teaching profession, but I was still frightened to death when it came to saying hello to her.

My academic prowess was, I suppose, okay for Parkfield, it being a school with a modest track record in getting people into the local grammar school. The high point of my primary education was in Class One with Miss Burgess, when in August 1955 I was third in the class exams and received a small book called *Stories of Robin Hood*, which I still have to this day. For the following three years I was somewhere in the middle of the class; not the best preparation for the eleven-plus examination at the end of Year Four.

I do not remember any intensive preparation for the eleven-plus, and I think the school only expected a few people to pass the examination, which was the case. The examinations took place over one day at Durnford Street School, with lots of children in a very large hall. 'Lambs to the slaughter' comes to mind when I think of it today. The arithmetical part of the examination was okay—at least I had half an idea as to what was being asked—but from then on it was downhill all the way. I vaguely remember thinking that the English and General Knowledge/Information papers bore no resemblance to anything I had done in my four years at Parkfield, hence my fate was sealed.

Not to try and make any excuses, but during my final year, my eyesight problems came to the fore, in that I sat in the middle for the class but could not see the blackboard. I coped by closing my eyes tightly and then suddenly opening them as wide as possible, and hey presto, I glimpsed what was on the blackboard for a fleeting moment. I suppose my experience of the eleven-plus examinations was typical of many children during the 1950s, and the critics were gaining momentum, the comprehensive eventually replacing the grammar and supposedly inferior secondary modern schools. There was a school of thought that the two-tier secondary education system created second-class citizens from a young age and lowered future aspirations, due to failure of the eleven-plus. Personally, I did not have any feeling of being left behind by failing the eleven-plus, mainly because all my friends had also failed. In fact, I knew very few people who actually passed the exam, one being Paul Grandige (decent goalkeeper) who lived on Sherbourne Road.

However, one thing is for sure: I will always be eternally grateful to Parkfield for introducing me to football and my love of the game, which I have retained to this day. I was reminded of my passion for football when, having recently failed miserably to improve my swimming abilities, my elder sister, Glenys (who is a good swimmer, having learnt at school), commented that I was "too busy playing football". What is it about football that becomes all-consuming from an early age? I played my football on the red rec, an unforgiving shale pitch, every lunchtime, and for me this was my 'Wembley', where my early dreams of becoming a footballer were acted out. After school, at 4pm, weather and light (in the winter) permitting, I would be out there playing football until it was time to catch the bus home. I particularly remember one day, when it had snowed in the afternoon and several of us decided to play football after school, the white of the snow and a clear sky gave the red rec a special sort of light that allowed us to play. Bordering onto the red rec were some houses on Factory Street that were no better than hovels, and one of the scruffiest and poorest families, the Stirrups, lived in one of these houses. On this particular day, Neil Stirrup emerged onto the red rec to play football, holding a pancake in one hand, wrapped in newspaper, and in the other, a cup of tea in a tin mug. I remember thinking, *Even we are not that poor to have to use newspaper and a tin mug.* I can still remember the boys I played with all those years ago: Tony Best, he of the unkempt blond hair, who played football with a passion that bordered on the reckless at times, and was a decent goalkeeper; John Priestley, who was much more serious about playing football, and was a reliable and solid defender; Colin McMullen, a diminutive player with a good 'football name' and excellent ball skills; tubby Michael Fallon, a sometime goalkeeper of decent ability; Jack Ramsden, not the greatest footballer, but a trier; and Philip Henshaw, being all arms and legs. To use a modern phrase, 'we did not have much strength in depth', and when playing on the red rec at lunchtime, we were usually beaten by the year below us. Their best players (the very best being someone called Anthony Foley) were much smaller than us, but could they play football! I always found this situation hard to swallow; after all, we were older and bigger than their players, and should have regularly beaten them. One of the highlights of my fledgling football career was when I was selected for the school team and we got to perform on the playing fields at Middleton Town Hall wearing proper football shirts. Cannot remember the score or who we played. My football journey was only just beginning at Parkfield, but it had given me the first taste of the 'beautiful game'.

One of my best friends at Parkfield was Billy Hardiman, who had two sisters who were friendly with my elder sister, Marlene. Billy was a good lad (not a footballer), and we developed an enduring friendship during the four years of our junior education. He and his family still lived in the centre of Middleton, close to Marsh Row where I used to live, in those terrible back-to-back slums more typical of the Victorian era than the middle of the 20th century.

Another friend was Freddie Mottershead, who came from a tough family and was, as you say, 'cock of the school', always skilfully using his fists in fights; the days of kicking people in the body and head were in the future. Also, I remember Freddie for his prowess at conkers, as every Autumn they would fall from the trees and there would be a mad scramble to find the biggest and best conkers. Several days of preparation ensued, involving the hardening of the conkers, ranging from cooking them in the oven to soaking them in vinegar. The big day arrived when everyone came to school with several conkers of different shapes and sizes, and battle commenced. Over a period of days, many conkers would fall by the wayside, smashed to bits by the battled, hardened champion conkers, some having fought 20 or 30 battles. Freddie always seemed to have the winning conker, it being somewhat gnarled and misshapen after many battles but remaining as hard as nails. Freddie and I both progressed to Hollin County Secondary School, and we remained friends for a number of years. I remember meeting him many years later in the local pub after he had been invalided out of the paratroopers and thinking how exciting his life was compared to my own at the time. Freddie had an older brother called Danny, a much tougher nut than him, and I think he also ended up in the army. The Mottersheads lived in a truly awful house in Middleton, tucked away from the town centre in a small dingy street; my enduring memory being of the cold, hard, grey, slate floors, and not a carpet in sight.

Parkfield was a Church of England school with strong links to Parkfield Holy Trinity Parish Church. At certain times of the year we all had to attend various church services, none of them remotely interesting, or even meant to be. My vague recollections are of the vicar being unable to make any connection with the pupils. Something related to the church that has remained in my memory for the past 60-odd years is the time when Woolworths opened a store in Middleton. This was an exciting event in those drab post-war years, and was looked forward to by both my friends and me. Unfortunately, the 9am opening time coincided with Ascension Day, which meant a day's holiday; BUT before this could be taken, there was a service at Parkfield Church to endure. There was much shuffling of bottoms and feet in the pews as everybody was willing the interminable service to be over so we could all run as fast as possible to the new store. Everything that day was sixpence (old money), and with my silver coin, I surveyed 'the wonder of 'Woollies' and purchased a pack of toy soldiers. My contact with the church also involved attending Sunday school, which involved a lot of singing and reading of the Bible—not really my cup of tea. Needless to say, my attendance did not last very long.

I cannot remember exactly when I became interested in girls, but I can remember their names: Anne Dewhurst, Margaret Hicks and Jacqueline Edwards. All three girls were, in my young eyes, very pretty, well dressed and near the top of the class—these being important factors in the grey and colourless days of the 1950s. My favourite was probably Margaret Hicks, who lived just off Higher Wood Street, which bordered the burgeoning Langley Estate. She was unattainable in many ways, and on occasion my way home passed her house, and I was always hoping to see her—not that she would have noticed me. Upon leaving Parkfield School I lost touch with her, as she went to Durnford Street School, although I did see her on the Number 17 bus several years later. I don't think she recognised me. Anne Dewhurst was the first girl I kissed (only once), and this took place behind the football changing rooms at Middleton playing fields. Afterwards, I raced off home thinking this was the best day of my life. Anne lived in one of the posh parts of Middleton, near to the town hall, which was a few minutes' walk from the town centre. Her father was a policeman, and partway through her time at Parkfield he was transferred to Seaforth, near Liverpool (what a memory), and she promptly disappeared from my conscience. Jacqueline Edwards was what you might call 'my first or second reserve', in that she lived on Sherbourne Road, this being the next road to Pershore Road, and I suppose I kissed her a lot, simply because she was always available.

We were a relatively poor family (by no means the poorest), but it was sometimes the seemingly inconsequential situations which reminded me of how poverty can manifest itself. During my time at Parkfield, my mother made almost all my clothes, and due to her rag-trade skills, she made such things as my shirts, trousers and coats and then knitted my pullovers, gloves and woolly hats, but she did not make underpants! In the 1950s the fledging NHS were spreading their wings, and this involved regular medical examinations to check the general health of children. The NHS duly arrived one day, and as we were all lined up awaiting our turn to be examined, the nurse told all the boys to take off their clothes, leaving everyone in their underpants. Shock horror! I did not have any underpants, as I had never worn underpants. For a few moments I was in a state of complete panic, viewing the prospect of taking my trousers down with utter dread. Fortunately, the nurse noticed my agitated state and quietly spoke to me, resulting in my examination being done with my trousers on. Needless to say, I informed my mother of my experience, and she somehow managed to find the money to buy me my first pairs of underpants.

Free dental care was another result of the NHS formation, but the problem was that you had to attend the local clinic (very few private dentists) for any treatment. Unfortunately, the few people who did attend the clinic embellished their experience with stories of brutal and painful treatment carried out by a sadistic dentist wielding a pair of plyers to wrench teeth from bleeding gums while the patient was strapped into the dental chair! Needless to say, this deterred many children, including myself, from seeking treatment in my primary school years, and this contributed to the poor state of my teeth for many years, only being saved by a relatively inexperienced junior dentist from Africa when working at the CWS in the 1960s.

Another thing which reminded me of my social status was the use of the term 'Sunday best' in relation to the clothes we wore. During the week, I would wear my everyday clothes, and then only on a Sunday did I get to wear my better clothes, or my Sunday best. For a number of years, I wore my Sunday best for the regular visits to my mother's parents who lived in Hollinwood, near Oldham, and it was always important to my mother that we did not dress like 'the poor relations'. The concept of 'best clothes' has stayed with me all my life, and even to this day if I buy new clothes, I am reluctant to wear them immediately, sometimes waiting for a special occasion.

I have some clear memories of the visits to Hollinwood, particularly the variety of buses used. One route involved taking a double-decker bus to Middleton Junction, at which point we had to leave the bus and then wait for a single-decker to continue our journey, as the bus had to pass under a low railway bridge. Coming home we would take a different bus, waiting for it on Broadway, which then took us back to Middleton by another route, avoiding the low railway bridge. Buses were the responsibility of local councils, and each town had their own colours, with Rochdale blue, Oldham purple and Manchester red. Don't ask me why, but I always wanted to travel on a Rochdale bus; maybe it was that they appeared cleaner and they were a wonderful light blue in colour.

My sisters and I also regularly visited my grandparents (Ellen and Henry Cooper) during the school holidays when my mother was at work. We had to make our own way to our grandparents by bus; not something that would happen today, as we were all relatively young. There was not a lot to do at our grandparents', and my abiding memory was a tin box with wooden bricks inside; I spent many happy hours playing with them on the kitchen table. There was no back garden, only a small backyard to play in, so my sisters and I spent our time exploring the nearby allotments. Although my grandparents were very welcoming to my sisters and me, there was always the feeling that we were viewed as second-class citizens, due to our family circumstances, and, therefore, treated sympathetically by the wider family.

In the late 1950s Middleton did not offer many things for young people to do during their leisure time, an important aspect being the existence of three cinemas. The first cinema was the Empire, which opened in 1860 as a variety theatre and managed to survive for over a hundred years before widespread TV ownership signalled its demise. For me the Empire was a bit of a puzzle, in that I hardly ever went to see a film there, viewing it as a place where they showed too-serious films.

The Victory and the Palace were more to my liking. The Victory (known as 'The Bug House') was, as you can guess, the poor relation of the cinemas in Middleton. It was situated on Wood Street and was built in 1870, starting life as a chapel before converting to showing films in 1910, but still retaining the pews as seating. The best thing about The Bug House was the Saturday morning for children, when they showed all kinds of films, my favourite being *Flash Gordon*. The Palace was the posh cinema in Middleton, located in the centre of the town, across the road from the 'Pee Gardens', and showed all the most recent films. You definitely had to behave yourself when at the Palace; any noise or bad behaviour resulted in immediate ejection by a very smartly dressed usher.

A special treat was a visit to The Avenue Cinema, situated between Middleton and Manchester. This cinema was a cut above the ones in Middleton, and appeared, to my young eyes, as enormous in size. If you were lucky enough to have a girlfriend, this was definitely the place to take her, provided you could afford the bus fare and ticket prices.

Holidays were an important part of my early life, and despite the sometimes harsh conditions of post-war Britain, my parents still managed to take the family on an annual two-week holiday. Middleton was a cotton town, as were the other surrounding towns, and every August the cotton mills closed down for what was called the 'Wakes Weeks'. The favourite holiday places for the people of Lancashire were either Blackpool or North Wales, and they flocked to these areas in their hundreds of thousands in the 1950s and 1960s. Not many people had cars in this period and, therefore, relied upon public transport—either railway or coach— to get them to their destination.

For us it was always North Wales and the immediate area around Rhyl. I can vividly remember the excitement of the Saturday mornings when we made our way to the railway station in Middleton to board the steam engine for our journey. The station was always incredibly busy on such days, with several trains leaving in quick succession to their respective destinations. The excitement as the steam engine entered the station was palpable, and for a young boy like myself it was, on occasion, just too much; my mother told the story of my frantic kicking of her legs in excitement, which left them black and blue. Needless to say, on the return journey I was wearing plimsolls!

The journey to North Wales took us through the industrial heartlands of Lancashire and then on to the coastal plain of North Wales, where we first saw the sea—a wonderful sight, and something which we would only experience once a year. The train stopped at several stations along the coast, and we normally alighted at

Abergele and then took a taxi to wherever we were staying, which was usually a caravan site. Such sites dominated the coastal road from Abergele to Rhyl, and then on to places like Prestatyn. They consisted of hundreds of caravans on a site, with various facilities ranging from penny arcades to outside swimming pools.

We almost always stayed at a small caravan park called Glan-y-Don at Kinmel Bay, which was halfway between Abergele and Rhyl. It was run by Mr and Mrs Nightingale, who lived on the site. Their site was unusual in that there were very few actual caravans there; we as a family stayed in what was once a railway carriage, with not many mod cons; very much the days of outside chemical toilets. A couple called Mr and Mrs Donachie were always regular visitors to Glan y Don, and their accommodation was basically a shed; talk about no room to swing a cat. I can still see Mr Donachie leaning over the side of the lower half of the door smoking his pipe.

Although the Donachies were much older than my mother and father, we all became good friends, and the Cooper family went to visit them in Birmingham; another exciting train journey, although by then I had stopped kicking my poor mother.

Jack Nightingale was a larger-than-life character, and must have been in his sixties at the time. In addition to maintaining the site, he was also the local Punch and Judy man at the nearby, much larger, caravan site of Palins. He also organised many games for the children at Glan y Don, which by today's standards would appear to be somewhat tame, but this was our two-week holiday and we were determined to enjoy ourselves, so we threw ourselves into such games with gusto. Most evenings Mam and Dad would go for a drink at the club on Palins, and so we were left very much to our own devices—something that would not happen in today's modern world.

A mobile fish and chip van would come to Palins several times a week, and my sisters and I would usually share a bag of chips back at our railway carriage, complemented by a large number of silverskin onions!

Further down the road from Palins was another caravan park called Oakfield, which had a small cinema—a simple pleasure by today's standard, but an integral part of our holiday in those days. I remember what seemed to be a great adventure when Alex Hartshorn, a family friend who was on holiday with us, and I went to the local beach one beautiful sunny evening and came back with all sorts of things, shells and tiny creatures, which we had collected. We could not wait to go back the next morning to explore further, but the sun had gone, replaced by a grey day, and the tide was so far out, making it appear completely different from the previous magical evening.

I think my father came on holiday under a certain amount of sufferance, as having only one leg did not lend itself to playing with my sisters and me on the beach, so he tended to find himself a local pub with a bookies nearby (usually in Rhyl), and that was generally him done for at least the afternoon. It was then left to my mother to keep us occupied, which she did without any apparent signs of resentment towards my absent father.

One year we decided not to go to Glan y Don, as my mother had seen a cheaper holiday in the local newspaper at a place called Talacre, which was near Prestatyn, just down the coast from Rhyl. It was a big mistake, in that Talacre was a very small place by the sea at the end of a long narrow road, the accommodation was not very good, and we were a long way from 'civilisation', in terms of the local pub and the bookies for my father. Needless to say my mother never heard the last of this from my father for some time, and we did not go to Talacre again. Many years later, on a trip down memory lane, I visited Talacre, and I don't think much had changed apart from the posh manner in which people pronounced the name of the place.

On the beach near Rhyl with
my mam and sister, Marlene.
Think I want an ice cream?

On the promenade at Rhyl
with my mam and sisters.

At the Jack Nightingale Punch and
Judy show at Palins Holiday Camp. I am the
one with the blond hair and white shirt.

Maybe the Talacre disaster prompted us to look elsewhere to spend our holidays, and I suppose we thought we were going upmarket when we started going to Butlin's in the late 1950s. Billy Butlin had started his holiday camps in the late 1930s, but the advent of World War Two saw them transformed into army camps, and only after 1945 did they start to return to their former state. The Butlin's camps offered somewhat more than caravan holidays, with people being housed in chalets with all mod cons, and was possibly the original all-inclusive holiday, without the booze. There was always something to do, regardless of the British weather, both indoors and outdoors during the day, and at night there was good holiday entertainment organised by the famous Butlin's Redcoats. Several of these Redcoats went on to successful careers on the BBC and ITV, including Jimmy Tarbuck, Roy Hudd (better known in those days as 'The Hairy Fairy') and Des O'Connor. The sites were scattered all over the UK: Filey, Skegness, Pwllheli, Clacton, Bognor Regis and Minehead. Initially, we travelled to the northern camps, they being a bit closer to home, with shorter travelling times, and by then coaches were very much the order of the day. Eventually, we became more daring and travelled south to Clacton, situated on the Essex coast; quite a journey by overnight coach to make sure we were there on Saturday morning, ready to occupy our chalets from midday, and that we did not miss a minute of our precious one-week holiday. I remember when we ventured as far south as Bognor Regis on the south coast in 1960, and travelled by train, first of all to London, and then on to Bognor Regis. We left Manchester in the early hours of Saturday morning, arrived in London at approximately 6am, a bacon buttie and cup of hot tea being our breakfast, and then we waited a few hours for the train to Bognor. It was hard for my mother to cope with the journey, as my father could not carry any suitcases, so even to this day I am still not sure how she managed; but she always did, because she was that sort of person.

Bognor Regis was a relatively new camp, being a cut above the other camps, and was a popular place for people to spend their holidays before the advent of the Spanish package holiday in the 1960s. An added thrill for me was to see the Tottenham Hotspur double-winning team at Bognor Regis, as they were there on holiday with their families; maybe this was a reward from the football club for making history the previous season by winning the First Division title and the FA Cup. I can still remember the Tottenham team: Brown, Baker, Henry, Blanchflower, Norman, Mackay, Jones, White, Smith, Allen, Dyson, and must not forget their legendary manager, Bill Nicholson. It was the dying days of the maximum wage, as players wages would dramatically improve in the coming years, and footballers would start to increasingly take their holidays in more exotic places, away from the prying eyes of the general public.

Bognor Regis was also the place where my career as a stand-up comedian briefly flowered, and then abruptly died. Talent contests were very popular at Butlin's Holiday Camps, and catered for both young and old. The children's competition was usually held in the afternoons, and aspiring young talent had the chance to sing and dance or whatever took their fancy; in my case it was telling jokes, and hopefully being funny. I was, in fact, the only person telling jokes, and everything was going well, with lots of laughter at my jokes and my 'strange' northern accent. Then I made the fatal mistake of telling my black and white parrot joke! The joke was about a little old lady who had two parrots: one black, which was always swearing, and the other white, which never did anything wrong. The little old lady always took the white parrot to church with her on Sunday, but would not take the black one, for obvious reasons. However, one week the black parrot decided that he was going to church instead of the white parrot, so he painted himself white and the white parrot black. Unknowingly, the little old lady went to church with what she thought was the white parrot, and the vicar started the service with the words "Stand up. Stand up for Jesus", at which point the 'white' parrot said, "Sit down. Sit down for Jesus. The buggers at the back can't see." This, I thought, was the icing on the cake, as it brought the house down. Little did I know what was to come. Just before the results were announced, I was taken to one side and told that I had been disqualified for using bad language, the use of the word 'buggers' being the problem. I was flabbergasted at the time, but I suppose it was 1960s Britain, and I was 'down south'. The best bit was outside the theatre, with many people telling me that I should have won and to disqualify me was ridiculous.

PART THREE

FOOTBALL AGAIN

Football has and always will be a passion of mine, and it manifested itself in many different ways. Where do I start? Maybe, somewhat strangely, with Albion Rovers, a lowly Scottish team. In the late 1950s children did not have much to entertain them in the evenings, with TV being limited and very much focused on adults. I can genuinely remember, as if it was yesterday, when the thought came to me to invent my own football game. It was a Sunday evening, and I was sitting on the lino in the living room. Money was non-existent, so it was 'find your own materials', which consisted of sturdy, white, cardboard shoeboxes, plasticine, buttons and a small box of paints. The white shoeboxes were used to draw the players, complete with shirts, shorts and socks, which were then cut out and painted; cannot remember the colours I used. Buttons were then selected, courtesy of the many boxes accumulated by my mother over her many years in the rag trade, and the player was then affixed to the button with a blob of plasticine. My creation was amazing in my young eyes, and my first team was named Albion Rovers. To this day I cannot remember why I chose this team, although some Scottish teams do have wonderfully evocative names; for example, Dundonald Bluebell. From these small beginnings, my new game mushroomed to over 50 teams, carefully stored in all manner of containers, including old Nescafé tins. At one point I ran out of buttons and had to be creative and use small square pieces of cardboard. I created several leagues for both first and second teams and kept meticulous records of the games, teams, scores and scorers. Information about players and their names was limited, and I relied heavily on the football magazine *Soccer Star*, now long since defunct. All games were played on the kitchen table using an old green woollen tablecloth marked out with my mother's marking chalk, once again courtesy of her job in the rag trade. The goals were somewhat rudimentary until my mother knitted me some nets, the ball being fashioned from a small piece of plasticine. This provided me with many hours of enjoyment, and I had to use my imagination to create the excitement for these games, with lots of self-commentary (better known as talking to myself, of which I had some previous history); and nobody was allowed in the kitchen while I was playing the games. I created my own heroes and superstars, one such player being Ken Knighton, who at the time was a reserve player for Wolves; he became my 'Roy of the Rovers', scoring lots of goals. Interestingly, Ken Knighton later joined my beloved Oldham Athletic and then had a relatively successful playing career with Preston, Blackburn, Hull City and Sheffield Wednesday, latterly managing Sunderland. Several of my friends, particularly Stuart Liddle and Dave Lavender, also played the game; some of them building their own stadiums from wooden fruit boxes, which included stands and floodlights. Indeed, my father suggested to me that the Subbuteo company (a famous football game) had stolen my idea, but I will never know.

Somewhere roundabout 1958, when I was 10 years old, I started going to watch football matches with my brother Donald, as he was a Bolton Wanderers supporter. Every other Saturday we would catch the bus to Heywood Railway Station and then take the train (still steam) to Bolton, and from the station we would walk the 20 minutes to Burnden Park. For a 10-year-old boy it was a magical time, as Bolton were one of the better teams in the First Division and were captained by the 'Lion of Vienna', Nat Lofthouse (the England centre-forward of legendary status). At the risk of boring anyone, I can still remember the team: Hopkinson, Hartle, Banks, Hennin, Higgins, Edwards, Birch, Stevens, Lofthouse, Parry and Holden.

It was in the year 1958 that Bolton won the FA Cup, although it was also the year of the Munich air disaster, and Manchester United, Bolton's opponents at Wembley, were much depleted after the deaths of their most important players: Roger Byrne, Duncan Edwards and Tommy Taylor. Two goals from Nat Lofthouse won the game for Bolton, his second goal being controversial, as he barged Harry Gregg into his own goal—something which today would have resulted in Lofthouse being sent off.

Night games under the floodlights at Burnden Park were always special, and one game that I particularly remember was against Wolves in the Charity Shield, which pitched the First Division champions against the FA Cup winners. Wolves were very much the best team in the league, with many England internationals, but were beaten comprehensively by 4–1. There was drama just before the game started, when Eddie Hopkinson, the England goalkeeper, was injured and could not play. The Bolton reserve goalkeeper, Joe Dean (somewhat surprisingly by modern standards), who was at home that night, received an urgent call from the club to come immediately to the ground, as he was required to play that night.

My dalliance with Bolton was relatively short-lived, as my brother got married and stopped taking me to the games. It was then that my lifelong 'love affair' started, and I had my Uncle Bill to thank for introducing me to the mighty Oldham Athletic, locally known as the 'Latics'. Uncle Bill was my father's much younger brother, who had had a difficult upbringing, his parents having died when he and his sister, Gladys, were quite young, which meant that they were both brought up by various aunts and family friends. He remained unmarried until he was in his thirties, and then married Mary, who was older than him and had two sons, Frank and George. She had previously been married to a soldier. His job was as a coalman, delivering coal in bags to people's houses five or six days a week, this being hard physical work. He always liked a drink and a smoke, and was partial to the odd bet on the horses— what you might call a true working-class northerner. I must say my experience of going to the Latics with Bill was somewhat mixed, in that he was almost always late in collecting me from our house, which meant we missed the first 10 to 20 minutes of the game, although Bill missed much more, as he spent most of the first half relieving himself in the toilet, after having consumed several pints in the pub before the match. His late arrivals to collect me really annoyed my father, and there were frequent arguments. Bill told me the story of my father being a regular Latics supporter for a number of years until there was an incident over a match ball. Latics, at each home game, raffled off the match ball, and one week my father had the winning ticket; so after the match he tried to claim his prize, only to be given a tatty old practice ball. He was told that he had no chance of getting the match ball, as they needed it for the next match. He then said that he would never go to watch the Latics, even if they turned up in the Lord Mayor's car for him, and he never did.

Bill had this wonderful old car. I think it was a Wolseley, which had the most efficient air-conditioning system: a hole in the floor of the car! At times, a somewhat daunting experience watching the road speed by underneath me from the comfort of my seat. Eventually, the police caught up with him, and he was prosecuted for an unsafe car and bald tyres. And he thought he had been badly treated by the officer involved, starting a heated debate outside the court.

Bill loved to tinker with his car, and was generous with his time in helping other people. One such instance was on a baking-hot Sunday afternoon in Oldham, when an old couple broke down in their car under Mumps Bridge, and Bill happened to be passing by. He immediately stopped, and over several hours helped to repair their car, which involved a trip to the local scrapyard for spare parts. The old couple were so appreciative that they nominated him for a Knights of the Road award.

Returning to the Latics, one of my favourite stories involving Bill was in August 1960, when he decided that we would go and watch them play in the first game of the new season at Chester in League Division Four. For me the first day of the football season was always a magical day, the previous season having been forgotten, whether it was good or bad, and inevitably the sun always seemed to be 'cracking the flags'. It was agreed that I would go to his house on Sunny Bank, a row of old terraced houses nestled behind the massive Warwick Mill in the centre of Middleton, for 11am on the Saturday morning, which would then give us enough time to reach Chester in time for the game. We were not travelling by car, as Bill's vehicle would not have made it there and back, so we would use the train from Manchester. Bill had been working on Saturday morning, delivering coal, and as usual could not resist the lure of a quick pint, so he arrived home late, covered in coal dust; so a hasty wash and a sandwich made by Auntie Mary, and we were on our way to Manchester by bus. On arrival in Manchester, we rushed over to Piccadilly Station, only to have just missed the 1.30pm train. His next thought was to go to Chorlton Street bus station to see if we could find a coach going to Chester. The only coach available was going to Llandudno in North Wales but was stopping in Chester. It was now about 2pm, and the match kicked off at 3pm, but as usual Bill was optimistic that we would get there on time. What he did not know was that the coach stopped several times en route to pick up passengers. We eventually arrived in Chester at 3.30pm, and then ran down Sealand Road to the ground, only to find all the entrances locked; and despite knocking on several doors, nobody seemed to hear us. Eventually, someone did hear us, and it was the Chester manager, Stan Pearson (also the old Manchester United star), who invited us into the directors' box to watch the second half. A difficult day was completed by Latics losing 1–0. Thankfully, the journey home was uneventful, although I remember the train home was late. *C'est la vie.*

My passion for Latics stretched beyond watching the first team every other week at Boundary Park, as there was also Latics Reserves to watch. I would catch the bus to Middleton, and then take the football bus to Boundary Park for another afternoon of football. Reserve teams in those days were a mixture of old, gnarled professionals and young, inexperienced players, with the occasional triallist, which brings me to Tommy Hutchinson. This particular day, Latics Reserves were playing Rotherham United Reserves, a team from South Yorkshire, on a wet and boggy pitch. Latics played a young triallist called Tommy Hutchinson, who was only 15 years old, having come from Dundonald Bluebell, a Scottish Junior team from the Fife area. In the first few minutes of the game Tommy received the ball on the left wing, and as the full-back, Owen Simpson, came charging into tackle him, he flicked the ball past him and was away down the pitch. I thought we had a star in the making, although Owen Simpson, a wily old pro, did not let him go past him again, with some robust challenges. Tommy went back to Scotland to eventually enjoy a very successful club and international career, starting at Alloa Athletic, then progressing to Blackpool, before moving to Manchester City, where he played in the 1981 Cup Final against Tottenham Hotspur and famously scored a goal for both teams.

The Latics team of the late 1950s was a mixture of seasoned professionals who were working their way down the leagues and young local lads hoping to make it in the professional ranks. The late 1950s had not been a great period for Latics, after the short-lived euphoria of promotion to Division Two in 1953 under the player management of George Hardwick, an England international who had enjoyed a long and distinguished career at Middlesbrough. The players I remember were Ivan Beswick, ex-Manchester United; the somewhat unreliable Dave Teece in goal; John Bazley, a local schoolteacher; and Peter Phoenix, who was eventually a member of the successful Latics team of the early 1960s. Other players were Jim Rollo, who took over in goal from Dave Teece, and a guy called Gerry Duffy, who was a 'bull in a china shop' centre-forward and loved to shoulder charge the goalkeeper from 30 yards out from goal.

From 1960 things started to change for the better at Latics, and the catalyst was the mercurial Bobby Johnstone, the archetypal Scottish 'tanner ball player'. Johnstone had been a member of the legendary Hibernian forward line of Smith, Johnstone, Reilly, Turnbull and Ormond, who terrorised Scottish defences in the 1950s. He then moved to Manchester City and was a member of the team which went to two consecutive FA Cup Finals in 1955, when they lost 3–1 to Newcastle United, and 1956, when they defeated Birmingham City 3–1.This game was famous for the City 'keeper, Bert Trautmann, breaking his neck during the game but courageously continuing to play on, unaware of his injury. Bobby then went back to Hibernian, but it did not work out for him, and Latics came calling. By the time Johnstone arrived at Latics, he was past his best, being somewhat overweight with 'dodgy' knees, and was prone to the odd drink or two. Nevertheless, he was still a potent force playing for Latics in the old Fourth Division. In Johnstone's first game, in October 1960, Latics beat Exeter City 5–2 in front of 17,116 spectators, the largest crowd for six years. Other players started to arrive: Ken Branagan and Bert Lister from Manchester City, Peter McCall and Alan Williams from Bristol City, John McCue from Stoke City, and Bob Ledger from Huddersfield Town. In addition, Jimmy Frizzell arrived from Greenock Morton, who became both a long-standing player and later a very successful manager of Latics. Another significant arrival was Jack Rowley as manager, a famous Manchester United player from the 1940s and 1950s. With this new team, Latics started to score lots of goals, playing entertaining football with Johnstone at the heart of the team creating lots of goals for his old Manchester City colleague, Bert Lister. Boundary Park started to see attendances of 20,000 plus for Fourth Division games, which even in those days was quite exceptional. I remember vividly a game in March 1961, when Latics played Peterborough United in front of 27,888 spectators at Boundary Park. Peterborough had only been elected to Football League that season, and would go on to be champions of the Fourth Division, with a record number of points and goals scored. It was an entertaining game that would have graced the First Division, and a 1–1 draw was a fair result.

However, the game that has etched in my mind over almost 60 years was the January 1962 fourth-round FA Cup tie against Liverpool, who were then managed by the relatively unknown Bill Shankly. They were in the Second Division, and Shankly was building a team that would very soon win the First Division and eventually dominate European football. Players such as Ron Yeats and Ian St John had come down from Scotland, and along with Tommy Lawrence would provide the spine of Shankly's great team of the 1960s. Other players were Roger Hunt and Gordon Milne and a very young Ian Callaghan. I was 13 years old, but I remember catching the football bus to Boundary Park along with several friends, one as young as seven years old, and then queuing to get into the massive open terrace at the Rochdale Road end of the ground. The price entering the ground was sixpence (two and a half pence in new money). Once in the ground, we stationed ourselves behind a barrier in anticipation of a great cup tie. What we had not realised was the size of the crowd that day, and as the ground filled up, we were 'pinned' against the barrier and started to feel the pressure of the crowd on the terracing, which was predominantly from Liverpool. We became frightened, and eventually moved to the side of the terracing where there was less pressure, our view now being somewhat obstructed. Nevertheless, what an atmosphere, with 42,000 spectators in

Boundary Park, and Latics did not look out of place against their more illustrious neighbours. There were no goals in the first half, and then Ian St John scored two quick goals in the last 15 minutes (one was definitely not a goal, as it hit the bar and bounced away from goal). Latics hit back with a Johnny Colqhoun goal with six minutes remaining, but that was not enough. During the game, a wall at the other end of the ground collapsed due to the pressure of the spectators, causing, mercifully, only minor injuries—a portent of things to come in the following decades.

In the following 1962–3 season, Latics went on to finish runners-up in the Fourth Division, and were duly promoted to the Third Division. The following season saw Les McDowell (ex-Manchester City manager) take over from a rather unfortunate Jack Rowley, and Walter Griffiths (again ex-Manchester City) become club secretary, with Bernard Halford going the other way, where he would enjoy a long and successful career at City.

The 1963–4 season got off to a decent start, having retained the majority of the players from the previous season, the early highlight being a 2–0 win against high-flying Coventry City, who were managed by Jimmy Hill. Hill was a Fulham player and formerly head of the Professional Footballers Association, having played a major part in the removal of the iniquitous maximum wage. The second half of the season was disappointing, and injuries, compounded the lack of depth in the squad, saw Latics finish ninth in the table.

Bobby Johnstone, my boyhood hero, managed to play 34 games that season, but sadly age and injuries were starting to catch up with him, and the following season proved to be his last for Latics. Bobby did like a drink, having been part of the infamous Manchester City 'drinking club' of the mid 1950s. Many years later a friend of mine, Roy Higginson, recounted a boozy story about Bobby. Roy and his wife were driving over the moors between Yorkshire and Lancashire, on what was a misty winter's morning, when ahead of them they saw this figure in the middle of the road swaying from side to side. It was Bobby. Apparently, he had been playing pitch-and-toss at a remote farmhouse, and in a somewhat inebriated state he was trying to make his way back to Oldham. Roy kindly gave him a lift home, for which Bobby thanked him and then casually mentioned that he was playing for Latics that afternoon. This would not have happened today. Indeed, I can personally vouch for the use of alcohol by footballers prior to games in those far-off days, as I would stand outside the dressing room at Boundary Park, waiting for players' autographs, and could smell the beer on their breath.

One of the pleasures of following football in this period was the weekly sports paper *The Saturday Pink*, which was published in the Manchester area immediately after all games finished on a Saturday afternoon. I would make my way down to the local newsagent's at 5.30pm, and along with many other people would await the arrival of the paper. *The Pink*, as it was called, would have all the results, plus local match reports, with a stop-press space for results that had not been included in the main body of the paper. The paper had some pre-written articles, but the putting together of the results and match reports must have been a logistical nightmare, as the telephone was the only method of communication they had. My earliest recollection of this type of newspaper was in the late 1950s when leaving Burnden Park with my brother and seeing a mobile printing van selling the Bolton version of *The Pink*, which was, in fact, green in colour. Once again, with the benefit of hindsight, a truly amazing feat in those far-off days of almost zero technology.

While I was growing up in the 1950s, there were still many of the great post-war players still plying their trade in the Football League, and the two most famous were Tom Finney and Stanley Matthews. It was always my ambition to see both of these players in action; fortunately, I saw Finney in action, but was not so lucky with regards to Matthews. The Finney game was at Deepdale on 18 April 1961, when Preston North End played Bolton Wanderers in a disappointing 0–0 draw. He was coming to the end of his illustrious career, but you could still appreciate why so many people saw him as one of the great English footballers. Finney was a loyal servant to Preston North End, and played for them all his career, but his resolve was tested in 1949 after returning home from an England game against Italy. England had won 4–0, and Finney was Man of the Match, which brought him to the attention of the president of Palermo. He was offered a lucrative contract to play for Palermo, including a £10,000 signing-on fee, a £100 per week wage (he was paid £20 per week at Preston) plus a villa and sports car for his and his family's use. On his return to England he met with his chairman, who in no uncertain terms told him that he could not join Palermo, and if he persisted in this request then he would play in Preston Reserves for the rest of his career.

With regards to Matthews, it was what you might call a near miss, in that he was playing for Stoke City (for the second time in his career), and in the 1962-3 season, they were firmly on course to win the Second Division Championship when they came to Bury at Gigg Lane on Wednesday, 14 May 1963. The local newspapers were full of 'the story' that this was probably the last chance to see the great man in the flesh, as he was 48 years old, the question being how long would he continue to play? So my friends and I caught the bus to Heywood, and from there on to Bury, before completing our journey on foot to the ground. Gigg Lane was bursting at the seams in the hope of seeing Matthews in action, and then came the big let-down, when just before the match it was announced that he would not play, due to injury. The disappointment was audible, and I have always believed that it was a con, and that there was no intention of allowing him to play in this game—who knows?

Talking about famous players, I also met a man who had scored a penalty in an FA Cup Final, his name being George Mutch, who scored in the 1938 Final for Preston North End. How it came about was when my cousin George was working with him for the local council, cutting the grass on our estate. (By the late 1950s his football career was finished, and sadly he had sold his winners' medal several years before, now being reduced to working for the local council.) My recollections of meeting him are a little hazy, but I clearly remember him showing me his shin bones, which after many years of being kicked all over the football field had moved to the side of his leg.

There were many footballers in this era who had wonderfully evocative names, one in particular being Armour Ashe. This player started his career at Aberdeen, and developed a reputation as a fearsome full-back, built like a tank and as broad as he was tall. He then moved down to England, playing for several clubs before ending up at Gateshead. I was at Boundary Park when he played for Gateshead against Latics in the late 1950s, where he showed that he had not lost his fearsome persona—but my God, he was so slow. He eventually died at the incredibly young age of 43, in 1968. Lloyd Lindbergh 'Lindy' Delapenha was another player from this era; what a wonderful name. He was the first Jamaican to play football in England, playing for Portsmouth and Middlesbrough, and I saw him play during the latter part of his career with Mansfield. On his retirement he returned to Jamaica and enjoyed a successful career as a journalist and broadcaster.

Televised football was almost non-existent in the 1950s and 1960s, and it was, therefore, difficult to keep up with what was going on in the wider football world. A real godsend was Saturday's *Grandstand* sports programme on the BBC, which was brilliantly anchored by the legendary David Coleman. One of its major features was the teleprinter service for football, which provided real-time updates on the football scores (the precursor to what we have today) as they evolved during the afternoon. This provided some magical moments in an era when there was so little football coverage. One incident which has lived in my memory was in February 1959, which was a day of heavy snow, and many matches were postponed. One game that survived was a fifth-round FA Cup match between Wolves and Bolton Wanderers, played on a snow-covered pitch at Molineux. Bolton were FA Cup holders, having beaten a depleted Manchester United (post-Munich) 2–0 in the 1958 Final, whereas Wolves were now the 'power in the land', due to United's demise. It was a truly heavyweight contest, and I avidly followed the first half via the teleprinter, being somewhat disappointed to see Bolton (my team at the time) going into the break 1–0 down. At this point a friend came to my house and asked ask if I wanted to play football, albeit on the snow-covered area at the end of our road in failing light. It was magical in my young eyes, as I imagined myself as Nat Lofthouse, the Bolton centre-forward, playing against Billy Wright, the legendary Wolves and England centre-half, hoping that I could win this 'game' with my friend; and Bolton would then win the real game at Molineux. On arriving home I saw the magical words on the teleprinter confirming the final score as 'Wolverhampton Wanderers: 1 Bolton Wanderers 2'—Lofthouse did score. Also during this time, there was a miserly 15-minute radio programme on Saturday lunchtime, during which there was a brief update on what was happening football-wise in the various regions of England. Larry Canning was the person who covered the Midlands, and I hung onto his every word when he told us if, for example, Ronnie Allen would be fit to play for West Bromwich.

Etched in my mind forever will be the Munich air disaster in February 1958 involving Manchester United. They were returning from a European Cup game in Belgrade when their plane crashed at Munich Airport while attempting to take off for the third time in bad weather. Several of the first team were killed, including Roger Byrne, Tommy Taylor and Duncan Edwards, these players also being the backbone of the England team at the time. The United manager, Matt Busby, was seriously injured, and at one time received the last rites from a Catholic priest before recovering to eventually lead the team to the European Cup win of 1969. For me there was a personal note to this tragedy, in that I was at a Cubs meeting on the Thursday night, the day on which the full horror of the crash became apparent. My mother insisted I still attend the Cubs that night, and one of my friends was Robert Fuller, who happened to be the cousin of Eddie Coleman, a young, outstanding United player who sadly perished in the crash. Robert was, like myself, 10 years old, and I suppose did not fully understand the magnitude of what had happened, so coming to the Cubs on that night was maybe his way of dealing with the situation. The outpouring of grief was enormous, via the newspapers, radio and TV, but overlaying all this was a stoicism of accepting the tragedy, given that it was only 13 years since the end of World War Two, when death and tragedy was an everyday occurrence.

Christmas was always a special time, and although we did not have much money, my mother and father always tried to make it a happy time. I remember one Christmas when I found my presents in a wardrobe, and to my great delight, for the first time in my life there was a football kit—shirt, shorts and socks in a luminous green and yellow. It bore no resemblance to any team I knew, but I loved that kit and wore it with pride.

PART FOUR

HOLLIN SECONDARY
MODERN SCHOOL

In September 1959 I started my secondary school
education at Hollin Secondary Modern. I had failed my
eleven-plus, and therefore was not able to go to
Middleton Grammar School, something which I was
not too unhappy about, as nearly all my friends were in
the same boat. Hollin was a new school, having been
opened for only two years, and catered mainly for
children from the Middleton council estate of Hollin,
although some children from the Manchester overspill
estate of Langley also attended. It was a Protestant
school, as opposed to the Roman Catholic schools of
Bishop Marshall and St Dominic's in the town, and as
they say 'ne'er the twain shall meet'; we just accepted
the fact that due to our religion we would go to separate
schools.

The first week at Hollin was taken up with exams to
establish in which classes the children would be placed,
and to my surprise I was placed in the top class, 1AA.
Hollin was a completely different school to Parkfield
in so many ways. It was a new school, and was much

bigger, with lots of space both inside and outside, and it took me a while to adjust to my new surroundings. There was a large school playing field with ample room for football, cricket, rugby and athletics, something which I was really looking forward to experiencing. However, the teachers were the major difference, in that there were a large number of them, and in the main, they all appeared to be relatively young and somewhat relaxed compared to the much older and straight-laced teachers at Parkfield.

The 1960s were just around the corner, and the winds of change were certainly starting to blow through the UK, with schools being no exception. The headmaster was Ross Schofield, a person who I was not entirely sure what to make of during my time at Hollin; a somewhat gruff individual who I think essentially let the teachers get on with things, and did not interfere too much. His deputy, Maurice Brunner, was a person who I liked very much, and appeared to run the school, the complex timetabling of lessons being one of his many attributes. Speaking of timetables, we all carefully copied our lesson timetables (no photocopying machines), and my five-year journey began, the first thing being to get used to the teachers.

Edgar Buckley was our maths teacher, who could be quite volatile, especially if he thought you were not listening. Miss Bolton took us for English, and was in our young eyes very glamorous. Brain Hall was the history teacher, who we called 'Caveman', on account of him being a somewhat hairy person. Tony Rogers was our geography teacher, who appeared to be a laid-back type of person—definitely one of the new breed of teachers. Tom Lowes (also known as Joe?) taught us the sciences with what appeared to be a distinct lack of enthusiasm. PE, not one of my favourite activities, was the domain of Brian Langan, who later in life became a good friend of my sister Marlene. George Grundy was the metalwork teacher; a rotund little man who had previously worked at an approved school and was not someone to be messed with, as I found to my cost on a number of occasions. The woodwork teacher was Eric Fallows, who I think was married to one of the other teachers, and was the complete opposite to Mr Grundy. Music was the province of Tom Corcoran and Gordon Niven; a subject I enjoyed, although I was not particularly good at singing or understanding music. Then, there was French, a relatively new departure for secondary school pupils, with Mr Roberts providing the enthusiasm to this very 'foreign' of subjects. Geoff Fletcher was the geography teacher; a hard man, having been a Rugby League player in his youth, and once again a person not to be crossed.

One of my earliest recollections was when all the pupils at the school were subject to an annual eye test, courtesy of the ever-developing NHS, something which was not done at Parkfield. The optician was amazed at how badly short-sighted I was and could not believe how I had coped with this problem for so many years. Glasses were prescribed, and my mam took me to the opticians for my first pair of rather ugly NHS glasses. Jack Cartwright, the optician, was a member of the Cooper family, having been adopted by one of our relatives and going on to become a successful optician in Middleton.

He was a kind man, and always treated us in a respectful way, even though we were 'the poor relations' of the Cooper family. Armed with my glasses I now saw the world in a completely different light. It was wonderful. Little did I know that many years later, after a cataract operation, once again I would see the world through my 'new eyes'.

My classmates in 1AA and the wider Year One intake were a varied bunch of people, having come from different schools, but we all appeared to get along reasonably well, although there were 'lines in the sand' which had to be 'drawn' in my early days at Hollin. An example of this was the issue of who was 'cock of the year', involving one boy from Hollin and one from Langley. Freddie Mottershead was my friend from Parkfield, and he took a beating from a boy called Cliff Lignum, who was not averse to kicking as well as using his fists. The fight took place after school in a farmer's field, and a large crowd congregated for the contest, which by the standards of the day was brutal. Fortunately, a number of the teachers got wind of the fight and arrived just in time to break it up and spare Freddie more punishment. Interestingly, Freddie and Cliff became good friends after the fight, a measure of respect having been established between the two of them.

Another person who I formed a fleeting friendship with was Ian McDougall, who I was surprised to see at Hollin, as I assumed he would have been going to Middleton Grammar School. His father, Harry, was a stalwart of Middleton Cricket Club, and the family lived on Hollin Lane, which in my young eyes was a posh place to live. Ian did not last long at the school, as the McDougall family moved to the West Country to run a post office. Several years later I saw him at Middleton Cricket Club, where he was playing while working in the area, although I do not think he recognised me.

Each pupil at Hollin was assigned to a house that during the school year took part in various activities to earn points, and at the end of the school year the house with the highest points was the winner. The house names were planets, and I was in Jupiter, the others being Mars, Saturn and Neptune. A large part of house activities revolved around sport, football being the most important for me, and I had an early morale booster to my fledgling house football career. I always played football in the school yard during break times, and even played on occasions with boys at least two years older than me. I must have impressed someone, as after only a few weeks I was approached by Pete Bradley, one of the house captains, to play for Jupiter in a house football match against older boys. Needless to say, I was excited to have been selected. House football matches were at that time played in the schoolyard, as the playing fields, even after two years, were not ready for use. It was a baptism of fire; playing in the schoolyard with your mates at dinner time was one thing, but the step up to house matches was an entirely different ball game. I think I was overcome by the occasion and did not play very well in the striker role, and was not selected again; my house football career being on hold for a number of years.

School dinners were much better at Hollin (did not like the onion gravy), as they were made on the premises, as opposed to Parkfield, where they were made at an outside kitchen and then delivered to the different schools in the Middleton area in large insulated containers to keep them warm. At Hollin we were seated in a bright and airy canteen on tables seating eight pupils, with the food served in metal containers, and everyone was entitled to one-eighth of the pie/ potatoes, etc. This worked well in the main, but there was a situation that put the fear of God into my friends and me in the first year. The boys in the fourth year were mainly from Langley Estate, and there was a certain group of them who we tried to avoid, particularly at dinner time. One of the group was a very small person, possibly with some kind of deformity. I cannot remember his name, but we nicknamed him Quasimodo from *The Hunchback of Notre Dame*, and if he happened to sit on our table, we knew it was not going to be good dinner time. If there was pie, we were not allowed to take our fair share, leaving a very large piece of pie for him, which he piled onto his plate with potatoes, etc., but invariably did not eat it all. Same went for the puddings, so were all mightily relieved when he and friends left the school at the end of our first year. Interestingly, some of his friends turned out to be good citizens, with one in particular, Vinnie Hindley, subsequently running a very successful business making muffins for Marks & Spencer. One story about Quasimodo which provided a sense of poetic justice was when he tried to jump off the local bus with his friends as it went up the hill on Hollin Lane. Unfortunately, the bus was travelling too fast, and he hit the road with an almighty thud, which his friends thought was funny.

In my later years at Hollin I stopped having school dinners and usually went home to eat, my mother trusting me not to burn the house down. However, this trust was sorely tested when I tried to use my mother's newly purchased egg poacher. I very carefully cracked the eggs and placed them in the circular containers ready for cooking. Unfortunately, I did not realise that you had to put water in the pan part of the egg poacher, and was somewhat frustrated that the eggs were not poaching very quickly. Eventually, a burning smell alerted me to the fact that there was a hole in the new pan. Needless to say, my mother was not best pleased.

The treat of the week was on Friday, when I caught the Number 163 bus to Middleton and went to Tommy's chip shop for fish and chips or a mixture consisting of chips and mushy peas. Tommy Thompson made the most wonderful fish and chips, and his shop was always full to bursting on a Friday dinner time, sometimes barely giving me enough time to eat my lunch and get back to school for 1.30pm.

In my early years at Hollin, the school published a magazine, which proved to be a lively source of information and debate. I was roped in to provide a monthly column on football, and decided to concentrate on the history of world football. Researching the information was not easy in those days before the Internet, and much of my information came from my trusty encyclopaedia on football, which was somewhat dated. In one of my early articles I made the bold statement that Sète was the oldest football club in France, which was immediately seized upon by our French teacher, Mr Roberts. He strongly contended that Le Havre was the oldest football club in France, the bone of contention being that Le Havre was indeed formed before Sète, but for a number of years, Le Havre played a game which was a cross between football and rugby. Letters to the editor followed, and for several days a lively debate ensued.

A successful part of the school's early development was the staging of several productions of the popular Gilbert and Sullivan comic operas. My elder sister, Marlene, was an excellent singer and was given the lead role as Mabel in the first Gilbert and Sullivan comic opera, *The Pirates of Penzance*. This was quite an undertaking for a recently opened school, and required a tremendous amount of work throughout the school to stage this production, which was then performed on several nights for both parents and children. Thankfully, usually everything went well on the nights of the performance, one of these being 9 December 1960, which was when the first episode of *Coronation Street* was televised. It was shown at 6pm, and I remember watching it and then having to leave with my mother to watch the evening performance.

My own school acting career then started to develop, and my first role was in *Wind in the Willows*, when I played Mole, which was only performed for the school. My burgeoning acting talents were duly noticed, and this led to a small part in the Gilbert and Sullivan production of *HMS Pinafore*, although I cannot remember my character. However, I then got a main part in another Gilbert and Sullivan production, *The Mikado*, as Koko the Lord High Executioner. It was quite a challenge having to learn lots of lines and sing several songs, but it was overall an enjoyable experience.

On the night of the performances I would like to think I performed to the best of my ability. The thing I found most difficult was learning the words for the songs, maybe because I was not such a great singer. I remember the frustration of Mr Niven, the music teacher, who was coaching me, especially when I sometimes forgot the words of the song. A very proud person at the nightly performances was my mother, who brought along several neighbours to see 'her beloved son', as my sisters called me. These performances proved to be very popular in the early years of the school, but sadly were not repeated during my later years at Hollin.

Part of school life was the seemingly constant round of injections for all sorts of diseases we might possibly catch. Needles were much thicker in those days, and there was very little compassion from the nurses, who seemingly, on an industrial scale, scarred our arms in the interest of getting the job done. What I always found particularly cruel was how we were sent for injections in groups of 10 pupils, and had to sit outside the injection room and emotionally suffer as people came out holding their arms with contrived, pained expressions. This did nothing for the well-being of the other pupils waiting for their own injections, and some pupils did not make it—cue the smelling salts.

I mentioned earlier George Grundy, the metalwork teacher; a rotund little man who had previously taught at an approved school and was not a man to be messed with.

The famous incident, which I will always remember was at the end of afternoon playtime. The boys were very slow at getting into their form lines before going back into school. This infuriated George, which resulted in all the boys having to come back to the playground after school. To our horror, George turned up with a huge slipper and proceeded to 'slipper' every boy on the backside. He started with the older boys, of which I was one, and then progressed to the younger ones. Needless to say, the power of his slippering was much greater for the older boys, and it certainly hurt, whereas for the younger boys it was less so, as slippering 200 boys eventually took its toll on George's right arm. The fallout from this action was zero in terms of complaints from parents, whereas if this had happened in later years, it would have been on national TV. Another incident with George was when I was close to leaving school and he was helping me make a companion set for the fire at home. We were walking from the school to the playing fields for the annual school sports day when I asked if he had managed to complete the companion set, to which I got a negative reply. I then said something along the lines of "Well, when are you going to finish it?" in an attitude which he clearly did not like, at which point he wacked me around the head, which almost knocked me into tomorrow. Needless to say, I said nothing further on the subject and retreated to lick my wounds, and certainly did not tell my mother, who in all probability would have said I deserved all I got. George did complete the work soon afterwards, which made me feel a little guilty.

Hollin was not a school at which I was ever particularly frightened by other pupils, despite the school-dinner situation, which was a short-lived issue, but there were a number of other incidents. Bullying was never much of a problem at Hollin from my perspective, but one incident, quite early in my time at the school, really did frighten me. There was a boy in my year called Micky Doran who was what you might call a 'hard nut', and I tried to avoid him. However, on this particular day I was waiting at the bus stop and Micky was also there, and he started to push and shove me, threatening all sorts of physical violence. I think he just enjoyed frightening me, and my God he did. When the double-decker bus arrived, he went upstairs, allowing me to escape downstairs, hoping that he would not notice me when he got off at his stop. The incident was never repeated, although I remained wary of him all through the years I was at Hollin.

There was another frightening incident, but in a very different way. It related to the Cuban missile crisis in October 1962, which was a scary few weeks for the world, and all the moreso for a 14-year-old boy. In the early days of the crisis all kinds of rumours were flying around the school, and one in particular was very unsettling. It centred around a boy called Ernest Bee, who was bright and intelligent but was somewhat of a maverick, with some odd views for someone of his tender age. This particular day, he was late arriving for the first morning lesson, which was held in the library, and quickly started telling everybody in hushed tones that the US had started firing missiles at Cuba and the Russians had fired back and we were on the verge of World War Three! There was no way in which we could verify this in the age of no mobile phones, and his news was taken at face value, causing absolute fear in the class and the wider school as the story spread like wildfire. At this point Geoff Fletcher, the ex-Rugby League geography teacher, took matters into his own hands and organised a series of discussions with all the pupils, explaining what the actual facts were at the time and how it might resolve itself in the coming weeks. He did not think the US or the Russians wanted another world war, and in the end, the Russians blinked and the missiles were removed from Cuba. Still cannot remember if Ernest Bee got the proverbial kick up the backside from Mr Fletcher, another man not to be messed with.

While at Hollin, I went on a number of school holidays, and the one that has always stuck in my mind was one to the South of France. The cost of the trip was £32, not an inconsiderable amount of money for the early 1960s, but it proved a real struggle for my mother to pay for the holiday, finally having to cash in one of her Liverpool Victoria 'penny policies' to ensure the money was available. These policies were literally what they said they were, in that people during the first half of the 20th century paid their 1p per week over many years, with some policies not paying out until 30 or 40 years after their start date. The policy documents were beautiful, ornate manuscripts, and many years later, when my mother died, I cashed in the remaining policies and asked Liverpool Victoria to send the policy documents back to me for framing. Unfortunately, Liverpool Victoria destroyed the documents by mistake!

Spending money for the trip was limited to £7, which by today's standards is a very small amount of money, but in the 1960s it bought you an awful lot. Funnily enough, I do not remember much of the journey from the UK to Arles, France, other than that we travelled by coach to Dover and then went on the ferry to Calais before transferring to a train to Paris and boarding the overnight train to Arles. I have a clear recollection of the couchette compartment for six people, although the small beds did not provide a good night's sleep. We arrived bleary eyed at a wet Arles the following morning and made our way to the wonderfully named Hostellerie De La Source. The hotel was run by a middle-aged couple who served up wonderfully wholesome food for the 10 days we were there. All meals involved a large amount of food, with the evening meal in particular being somewhat overpowering, even for hungry children. The soup was wonderful, and the cliché 'you could stand your spoon in it' was certainly true. The soup was then followed by chicken legs or meat, and mountains of chips, with no room for pudding. Cannot remember for sure, but I think we might have had the odd glass of wine with our meals.

My recollections of Arles are of a historic town almost untouched by heavy industry and very different from Middleton and its industrial past. Arles is described as 'the gateway to the Camargue', which is where the famous wild horses live, and on a trip to the region we saw these magnificent beasts in all their glory. In the Camargue area is the ancient city of Aigues-Mortes, which we visited—my recollection being of a walled city—and on the day we were there it was extremely hot. We also visited the seaside village of Saintes Maries de la Mer, and we, as the English, stuck out like sore thumbs on the local beach—having not heard of sun cream—with lobster red being the colour of the day. A funny incident occurred on the beach involving Mr Roberts, the French teacher, who had organised the holiday; he was seemingly propositioned by a young Scottish woman, and he looked very embarrassed with everyone watching him.

One thing I do remember is my introduction to the wonderful world of the Fanta Orange drink. I was sat at a café near the hotel after a long hot walk from Arles and was confronted by this wonderfully cold bottle of Fanta, that first taste having lived with me ever since. The weather in Arles was wonderful, but when we travelled back to Paris for the final two days, I think it rained for the whole of our time in the city and I only seem to remember the inside of the hotel room. We did eventually venture out into Paris and try out our faltering French. *Ou est the le cabinet*? was my famous phrase, which I thought meant 'where is the toilet?'. Needless to say, I was met by an incredulous expression from a French gendarme who had no idea what I was trying to say. It was a holiday I will always remember, and the Hostellerie De La Source is still in existence to this day.

In the 1960s certain subjects were very much for boys, and other subjects for girls, which caused a small problem when Mr Grundy (remember him?) was ill and away from school for several weeks, which meant there was no other teacher for metalwork. Therefore, we were taught domestic science by the wonderful Mrs Ratcliffe for a few weeks, which my classmates and I certainly enjoyed, giving us a chance to do some cooking, ironing and several other related activities. When Mr Grundy returned to school, we did not want to return to metalwork, but we had no choice, as it was what boys did in those days. I have always wondered what would have happened if there had been a choice between metalwork/woodwork and domestic science. Maybe my cooking skills would have been much better today, and I might not have burned a hole in my mother's new egg-poaching pan.

Having been in the top class, 1AA, from my first year, I managed to maintain this level for the whole of my time at Hollin, although expectations were not high in terms of what I might achieve. Failure of the eleven-plus along with my classmates meant that we were not expected to progress towards GCEs, as was the norm at Middleton Grammar School. Our ambitions were very much centred upon ULCIs (Union of Lancashire and Cheshire Institutes), the poor relation of GCEs but, nevertheless, something to strive for at the end of the fourth year. I cannot remember exactly what my position in the class was at the end-of-year exams, but I seem to recollect that I was consistently in the top 10, which gave me a certain level of satisfaction.

My classmates were a varied lot. Richard Other, who was by far the cleverest boy in the class (never quite understood why he was at Hollin). Jimmy Laffin (great name), who came from Langley Estate, was also a clever lad, and in later life had a successful business career but tragically died at a comparatively young age. Philip Booth was a friend of mine from Parkfield, and although we maintained a good relationship in the early years at Hollin, we drifted apart as we both went our separate ways. Jack Ramsden was also a friend from Parkfield School, his mother being the person who took us home from Parkfield during the 'pea souper' winters. Ernest Bee, he of the Cuban crisis, was potentially the cleverest boy in my class, but I suspect he could not be bothered. Wonder what happened to him. Another boy I remember was Cliff Lignum, who was a fascinating character. He was a handsome boy, always popular with the girls, a talented footballer (played for the Middleton Town team), generally accepted as the 'cock of the school', always fashionable, to the point of making the rest of us look 'very 1950s' in terms of our dress sense, and became a male model after leaving school.

Some of my friends were my football pals; in particular, John Tunnicliffe, Dave Lavender and Stuart Liddle who lived close to my home, and all three of them emigrated to Australia in the 1970s, although Stuart returned to the UK and sadly died a few years later. John was what you might call an elegant footballer—someone I always wanted to kick (sorry John). He went on to play for Hollang United, which was a amalgam of players from the Langley and Hollin estates, the divisions of the past forgotten. Dave was an awkward bugger to play against, being a feisty and competitive player, although I did not dare kick him. I met both Dave and John with their wives while in Perth, Australia, with my wife, Barbara, in 2014; and having not seen Dave for many years, the first thing he said to me was that he had last seen me in 1963 on the Number 17 bus. I was on my way to work at the CWS in Manchester, and he was going for an interview as a welder. What a memory! Coincidentally, there was another John Cooper who lived nearby on Nowell Road, him being called 'Slim John Cooper', with me being referred to as 'Fat John Cooper'. Slim John Cooper also emigrated, but to New Zealand, and sadly died in 2019.

I have not mentioned the girls, so let me try to remedy this oversight. Names such as Susan Croft, Fiona Murray, Marie Abson and Sheila McAllister come readily to mind; in particular, I remember Sheila, who I suppose I had a soft spot for. She and her family had moved from the North East, due to her father's ill health, and I remember him waiting for her at the school gates after rehearsals for the Gilbert and Sullivan comic operas. I suppose my first 'love' was Carol Simpson, who was in the class below me. I loved her from afar, never daring to approach her, as I was the little fat boy and she was totally out of my league, being willowy in stature, with beautiful long, black hair. Jennifer Holland was a year younger than me, and was someone I just fell totally in love with. There was a 'real pain' in this love, which was hard to cope with. She lived just around the corner from me, and I would walk home with her every day, aching for some recognition of my love for her, which was never really reciprocated. It got worse when she started to go out with other boys, one being Kenny Mulholland, a tough boy from Langley Estate who I was not about to challenge.

Linda Whitehouse was my first real girlfriend, and she had a twin sister, Janet, who was going out with Denis Wilson, a football friend of mine. It was at the time when I was performing in the Gilbert and Sullivan operas, and just maybe my relative fame had impressed her. I think Linda and Janet's mother must have been from outside of the UK, maybe Spain, as they were both olive-skinned and in a certain way were somewhat exotic creatures compared to the 'sheet white' natives. The relationship did not last long, although I do remember seeing her several years later. Sadly, she did not recognise me.

Another girl was Maria Baron, who lived nearby, and I was infatuated with her for a short period of time but could not communicate with her, resorting to frequently walking past her house in the hope of seeing her to say hello. Her mother was from Greece, and Maria was, in my young eyes, very beautiful. The situation came to a head when I followed her one day as she went to her grandmother's and must have frightened her. Unbeknown to me, her grandmother was a local magistrate, and Maria told me that if I followed her again, her grandmother would take action against me. Needless to say, I behaved myself from then on and remained on friendly terms with her.

Football was an important part of my time at Hollin. Most Saturday mornings were spent playing football on a small piece of land opposite the several local shops which were the focal point for the ever-growing Hollin Estate. It was an uneven piece of land which was not entirely flat, there being an upward slope to one end of the pitch. The goalposts were somewhat haphazard, with a small tree at one end being one goalpost and coats providing the others. There was not much grass on the small pitch, and on occasion the inclement weather made it into a mini-mudbath, and my mother was not best pleased when I showed up one day at the nearby bakery in a very muddy state.

In the main, I played with John Tunnicliffe, Dave Lavender, Stuart Liddle and Phil Craven, who we nicknamed 'Craven A' after the cigarette brand, along with various other boys. These games, despite the somewhat primitive conditions, were through the mists of time wonderful experiences, as it was just the sheer joy of playing the game I have loved all my life.

We also played on Sunday afternoon on a somewhat larger pitch with proper goalposts, with several teams from the estate taking part. These games were very physical, and winning was everything, so lots of cuts and bruises. The pitch was much better than the 'Saturday pitch', but it had one significant drawback: it was near to quite a steep drop leading to a small stream, so scrambling down the bank for the ball sometimes upset the rhythm of the games.

One of the teams was run by Mike Marsland, who was a local doctor's son. He lived in a very nice private house on the edge of the estate. Mike was not short of money, and on one occasion he approached me to play for his team, offering me the princely sum of 'ten bob'. As a poor northern lad, this was untold riches, and I quickly agreed; maybe I should have asked for more? Mike had approached other local players, and we all met at his house for a training session. The gardener had turned the large lawn at the rear of the house into a five-a-side pitch, replete with goals. I remember getting changed in the garage—we were not allowed in the house—the size of it being almost the size of our humble abode on Pershore Road. After the training there were fizzy drinks and cakes awaiting us in the garage, and I was beginning to think I could get used to this new life as a 'paid' player. Alas, after a few games, the payments and refreshments stopped, and I went back to my 'day job' of collecting the football from the stream. During the school holidays, we formed a team from Pershore Road, with team members being Geoffrey Middlehurst, David Hilton, Alan Penman, Neil and Ian Shoreman, plus Stephen Payne.

On one occasion we decided to play the much-feared Brassey Street team, who were based on the nearby Boarshaw Estate. They had some good players, namely Harry Stoddart and 'the twinners' (cannot remember their names), plus they also had a reputation for being a rough-and-tough team, and most other teams did not want to play them on their red shale pitch. So it was with some trepidation that we arrived at Brassey Street expecting the worst, we being a much younger team than them. We started confidently, and to our surprise we quickly established a 2–0 lead as we completely dominated the game. However, towards the end of the first half, Brassey Street started to 'wake up' and we struggled to keep them at bay, and it became inevitable that they would score sooner rather than later. Then the weather intervened, as there was a torrential downpour which completely saturated the pitch and the match was abandoned. We all ran home with the words of Brassey Street team ("We want to play you again very soon."), ringing in our ears. I think we all thought that our truncated 2–0 victory was as good as it was going to get, and playing them again would open up the prospect of an almighty hammering, so we decided to keep our heads down and hope Brassey Street would forget about the return match. However, they did come to Pershore Road to try and arrange another game, but we managed to avoid any commitment, and therefore our famous victory remained intact.

There were also games against the Slattocks village team during the school holidays. Slattocks was situated between Middleton and Rochdale, and so we would catch the Number 17 bus for the short journey to the village. Their team was mainly made up by sons of local farmers, and on their day they were a very hard team to beat. There was Denis and David Allison, the latter later becoming a Football League referee, John Fitton, who later kept goal for my beloved Latics, along with Derek, his brother (great left foot). Jock Smith, Ken Prideaux and John Partington were other players. The games were played on a pitch with goalposts by the side of the local canal, and we had to fish the ball out of the canal on numerous occasions. Sometimes we had to move cows from the field so we could play our games, but the minor hassle was worth it, as playing at Slattocks was always an enjoyable experience, especially when Mrs Allison provided much-needed refreshments after the games. Today the village has radically changed, with a huge motorway roundabout dominating the area, and our pitch is no more, with an industrial estate covering the area.

The pinnacle of my school football career came rather unexpectedly in the final year at Hollin. I was now captain of the school team, and our big game of the season was against Bishop Marshall, the Catholic school from the nearby Langley Estate. They were a formidable team, with their star player, Steve Moss, being an England Schoolboy international and someone who was apparently destined to be a professional footballer in the highest echelons of English football. In addition, Bishop Marshall had two Lancashire County players: Johnny Thompson and Steve McDonagh. The game was played at Hollin, and a decent crowd turned up to watch a game that we were not expected to win. I tossed up for the game with Steve Moss and decided to kick down a slight slope on a somewhat uneven pitch. As right-half (old money), I was marking Steve Moss and wondering what humiliations awaited me. Bishop Marshall scored early in the game, and we definitely feared the worst, although surprisingly I was managing to stifle Steve Moss to some extent. From being 1–0 down at half-time, we came back strongly in the second half, and with a few minutes to play, we found ourselves 3–1 ahead, thanks to some inspired play by a player called Tony Crolla. Bishop Marshall then scored to make it 3–2, and then we clung on for our life until the relief of the final whistle. Steve Moss was very gracious in defeat, and congratulated me and the team on a deserved victory. Unfortunately, Steve Moss did not become a professional player after brief spells at Blackburn Rovers and Bolton Wanderers.

In my time at Hollin a player emerged who was several years younger than me, by the name of Tony Hallam—a player of exceptional talent who went on to play for England Schoolboys. He was also a rather handsome young man, and has been married for many years to the sister of one of my football friends, John Tunnicliffe. His football career faltered after leaving school, and after spells with a number of professional clubs, he drifted out of the game. I do believe that if Tony had been born 40 years later and played in the era of the Premier League and Academy's, he would have made it as a professional footballer.

In my last two years at school, I re-established myself in the house football team, and in my final year Jupiter managed to win the house competition, with several of the school football team playing for us. Malcolm Kerfoot and Richard Oakes and I, being the school half-back line, were the backbone of the successful house team.

I was introduced to the formal game of cricket while at Hollin, and although it was not my favourite sport, I nevertheless enjoyed the odd game for my house team. My main interest was in watching Middleton Cricket Club, who played in the Central Lancashire League. Their ground was within walking distance of my home, and in those days Middleton played on a Saturday afternoon. Middleton, along with the other teams, were allowed to engage a paid professional player for the season, and, therefore, it provided an opportunity to see some of the best overseas players in the world. In particular, two West Indian players, Frank Worrell and Gary Sobers (both were subsequently knighted in later life), played in the League for Radcliffe, and I suppose when watching these wonderful players, I did not appreciate just how lucky I was to witness them playing. At Middleton we were fortunate to have two famous cricketers as our professionals, Roy Gilchrist and Basil D'Oliveira, during the 1950s and 1960s. Roy Gilchrist was a West Indian with a fearsome reputation as a fast bowler, who also liked a drink and lodged at the Crown Inn, the landlord being Alf Barlow, the Middleton wicket-keeper—not a good combination. A famous story about Gilchrist, which seems to have been airbrushed from recent cricket history, was when he was involved in bizarre incident when playing for Crompton (another Central Lancashire club) in the late 1950s. Crompton were playing Oldham, the Oldham captain being Bill Lawton, a well-known local cricketer who was the husband of Dora Bryan, the famous actress who starred in films such as *A Kind of Loving*. In those days cricket squares were not covered and, therefore, were open to the elements, which made for some very lively wickets. In the early part of the Oldham innings, Gilchrist hit one of the Oldham batsmen on several occasions with fast-rising deliveries, which caused the batsmen some pain. Attempts were made to calm the situation, but Gilchrist continued to bowl dangerously, at which point Bill Lawton called his players off the field and promptly declared their innings with a very low score. This meant Crompton would easily win the game, which as the saying goes 'was just not cricket'. This was big news in the local area, with Gilchrist being accused of being 'the wild man of cricket', and the following morning it was featured in the Sunday national newspapers.

The story of Basil D'Oliveira is well known, but maybe not many people will remember that it was Middleton who gave him his first opportunity to play cricket in England. D'Oliveira was South African, and being a Cape Coloured person, was only allowed to play cricket in the minor cricket leagues, due to the South African apartheid laws. This meant playing on very poor quality pitches, but nevertheless he developed a reputation as an outstanding local cricketer. He came to the notice of John Arlott, a famous English cricket commentator, who recommended him to several England counties without much success. John then contacted a man called John Kay, a local newspaper reporter in Manchester, who recommended him to Middleton. The club then sent him the airfare to bring him from South Africa to the UK. A poignant story on the day of his first game for Middleton was when he asked the club captain where his dressing room was, as he did not expect to get changed in the same room as the white cricketers. D'Oliveira initially found it very difficult to adjust to life in the UK, in addition to playing cricket on grass wickets, which he had not experienced in South Africa. However, he soon mastered the situation, and for a number of seasons became an outstanding local cricketer, which attracted the attention of Worcestershire, another county cricket team. The rest is history, as he was an outstanding player at Worcestershire and then made his England debut when he was in his early thirties, being a mainstay of the team as an all-rounder for several years. During his England cricket career, he was famously not selected for a tour of South Africa, due to the objections of the South African apartheid government.

School holidays while at Hollin were spent mostly at home with my two sisters, Marlene and Glenys. The local wood, Hopwood, was a popular place to visit, and in my young eyes was a veritable pandora's box of things to do during the long summer days. A stream ran through the wood, and on occasion my friends and I would camp overnight, something that today would not be a clever thing to do. Not much sleep was had during the night. It was very dark in the wood, and all kind of pranks would sometimes frighten the life out of us. The morning brought some relief, but burnt sausages did not improve the overall experience.

The wood had numerous tracks, some of which I knew well from my poor school-cross-country running performances, whereas others seemed mysterious, passing by isolated farms with barking dogs, which at times made me run faster than normal. A more familiar farm was the one owned by the Howarth family, which through my sentimental young eyes reminded me of the quintessential English farm, with a pond in the middle of the farm courtyard, replete with some very noisy ducks. On entering the wood there was a brick tower that rose from the ground to a height of approximately 20 feet. This was a part of the water overflow system which was built into the side of the hill and could be accessed by crawling into the overflow pipe which took you into a small chamber with a steel ladder, then up to the top of the brick tower. This was a game of 'dare', which my friends and I would undertake, going through the tunnel and up the ladder to the top of the tower, and then back down again. Unfortunately, my nerve did not hold, and on reaching the top of the tower I decided that I did not want to go back the way I'd come and decided to jump off the tower. Not a good idea! I landed face first, my nose bearing the brunt of the impact, and there was a lot of blood. I ran home covered in blood, and on being cleaned up by my mother, it became clear that the strip of skin separating my nostrils had become detached and was flapping around. Comfrey (a garden plant!) was applied, and hey presto, within a few days I was healed and back to normal, never to climb the tower ever again.

North Manchester Golf Club borders onto Hopwood, and lost golf balls were a welcome source of money, as we sold them back to the members. In the middle of Hopwood was De La Salle, a Catholic teacher training college, and they had several football teams of varying abilities. A game was duly arranged with the lads from Hollin Estate, and in view of our relatively young age, we assumed we would be playing one of their lesser teams. However, when we arrived at the college, we were told we would be playing their first team, one of the players being the brother of Pat Jennings, the legendary Northern Ireland, Spurs and Arsenal goalkeeper. The omens were not good! In later years we would have 'shut up shop' and defended for our lives, trying to frustrate the opposition and keep the score down to a respectable level. Unfortunately, we tried to take the game to them, and conceded several early goals. Discipline went out of the window, and several defenders abandoned their positions, the only honourable player being Brian Bentham, who continued to defend till the end of the game. I think the score was 24–0, and we never came remotely close to scoring a goal. Handshakes all round at the end of the game.

Trainspotting was very popular in the 1960s, as the age of steam was coming to an unfortunate end. Nevertheless, trainspotting at Slattocks railway bridge was a pleasure, and clutching my trainspotting book, I enjoyed many a happy hour spotting some of the most famous steam trains, including the Flying Scotsman. However, the railway bridge was the scene of another dangerous game, in that there was a stone ledge jutting out from the bridge structure overhanging the railway line. The dare was to walk across this narrow ledge platform with your back to the bridge wall. Several of my fellow 'spotters' completed the dare. Needless to say, after my experience in Hopwood I did not attempt it.

Miles Platting (a suburb of Manchester) was a place where the old steam engines were sent to be dismantled, and ultimately scrapped. In the early 1960s thousands of steam engines were being scrapped, and on one occasion I visited Miles Platting, better known as the 'graveyard of steam engines'. My memories of the day are not great, and the sight of all the engines on their 'deathbeds' was sad. Nevertheless, it gave me a last chance to 'spot' certain engines.

Memories of school holidays involve some of the most obscure things. I remember my cousin Gerald used to come to our house for his dinner, and on occasion, the most trivial things escalated into stupid situations. On one occasion, we were having peas with our meal and an argument started over how many peas we each had on our plates; it ended up with us counting the number peas on each other's plate. You could not make it up.

Pop, or 'mineral' as it was known then, was a rare luxury in those days, and my particular favourite pop was Ben Shaw's lemonade, the penny back on the returned bottles being a welcome source of extra money. With regards to 'pop', I remember when at a relative's house I mentioned that I was thirsty, whereby Uncle Jim said, "No problem. We have plenty of 'corporation pop.'" My joy was somewhat punctured when I found out that this was water from the kitchen tap!

During my early childhood my father was unemployed for periods of time, and when that coincided with the school holidays, he was in charge. His culinary skills were not the best, and dinner times were something to dread rather than look forward to. On one occasion my father presented us with something which was not particularly edible, and it was extremely slow going, as every mouthful was 'agony'. I assume my sisters managed to eat their food through gritted teeth, but my recollection was that I was determined *not* to eat it, and my father was equally determined that I *would* eat it. It was a long afternoon as we both sat there in the kitchen, but eventually he gave in and I was free to out and play with my friends.

During my later years at Hollin I started to play football with the Smith girls during the school holidays. The pitch on which we played being very much makeshift in nature, sloping from one side to the other. It was bordered by a small playground, replete with a roundabout and swings on one side and a dirt path on the other. Goalposts were non-existent, apart from one tree, so coats and pullovers were the order of the day. The Smith girls were talented footballers, and more than held their own against the boys. The younger sister was called Jane, the more attractive of the two girls, but Anne, the elder sibling, was much the better footballer, with good defensive qualities. The Smith girls lived on the corner of Furness Road and Hollin Lane in a nice detached house, their father Rod being a local businessman.

Despite the difficult conditions, there were many enjoyable games with people like Steve Brierley, Alan Norman and Denis Wilson, who was an excellent goalkeeper. After one of these games, Alf Wilson, the father of Dennis, commented that he thought I might make the grade as a footballer. Praise indeed.

Me in *The Mikado* as Koko the Lord High
Executioner wearing the cross.

Fame at last. I am a prefect.

School photo, *c.*1963, for Class 4AA plus the small number of fifth-year pupils. I am on the second row, third from the right.

School football team 1962–3. I am on the front row, second from the right.

Education at Hollin County Secondary primarily covered four years. The final year saw us taking ULCIs (Union of Lancashire and Cheshire Institute), definitely the poor man's version of GCEs. If I remember correctly, I passed all the exams, although how I passed French, I will never know. Part of the exam was to read a short passage of French and then answer questions on the subject. One word, 'Noel', figured prominently in the passage, and to my eternal shame I did not know this was the French word for Christmas, thinking it was someone's name. To this day I do not know what the examiner thought of my answers to the questions, with me babbling on about 'my friend, Noel'!

My time at Hollin was supposed to finish at the end of the fourth year, as the school was not geared up to provide education up to GCE level, this being the almost exclusive preserve of the grammar school. However, as the school developed during the early years, it became apparent that a small number of pupils were capable of undertaking GCE courses, and this started in the year above me. There were very few GCE pupils doing this first year, but I do remember two boys in particular: Walter Mills, the brother of Avril Mills (the first head girl at Hollin prior to my sister Marlene), and Raymond Wolfenden. Both of them seemed to me to be highly intelligent, and clearly should not have been at a secondary modern school; and they had that aura about them which I suppose I aspired to emulate. I assume their results were sufficiently good for the school to carry on with the 'experiment', and so I entered the fifth year of my secondary school education in September 1963.

A good proportion of my fellow pupils from Class 4AA joined me in the fifth year, and it was agreed that I would be entered for five GCE exams: maths, English, English literature, history and geography; definitely no science subjects. I think my mother was quite proud of me, as I was the only person in our family who appeared to be remotely intelligent enough to 'climb the academic ladder' and hopefully get an office job, thereby not having to 'get my hands dirty'. One consequence of staying on at school was that I was made a school prefect, having not been selected while in the fourth year. A shiny new prefect badge gave me a certain air of authority, which I endeavoured to use in a fair and consistent manner.

One of my jobs was to ensure that the transition of pupils from one class to another was done in an orderly and quiet manner, the main task being to make sure pupils formed an orderly and quiet queue outside the classrooms prior to lessons starting. On one of these occasions I came face to face with a boy who I had met briefly several years before, which was at the time a somewhat frightening experience for me. I was probably 13 years old, when one day I looked out of the front window of our house and saw a boy who was maybe two or three years younger than me ripping up and throwing newspaper all over the place, making a right mess of our front garden. I went outside, thinking that I was older and bigger than him and would soon sort him out. How wrong I was. The look in his eyes told me immediately that I was dealing with a very angry and aggressive person, and when I told him to stop what he was doing, his anger grew to such a level that I genuinely feared for my safety, so I retreated back into the house.

I do not remember coming across this boy in my previous years at Hollin, but now there he was, and I was pretty sure that he remembered the confrontation from a few years before. Needless to say, I gave him a wide berth for the remainder of my time as prefect, but in later years I wondered what became of him; either a career in the military, hopefully to channel his anger in the right direction, or prison, probably for murdering someone!

Another consequence of now being in the fifth form was that I did not have to wear school uniform anymore. I, therefore, decided that I would try to be a bit different in what I would wear for school during the next 12 months. I persuaded my mother to buy me a pair of brown corduroy trousers with a brown corduroy jacket to match, although the family budget did not stretch to a pair of brown shoes. Nevertheless, I received several comments about what was at the time my somewhat daring dress sense.

My school football career continued, even though the year below me had some excellent players, and I captained the school team on a number of occasions, including the famous 'Steve Moss' game. I cannot remember much about the academic year. Taking GCEs was a leap in the dark for both my teachers and me, and with hindsight it was probably akin to 'the blind leading the blind'. I was never quite sure how I should be preparing for the exams, and I suppose in the end this contributed to a disappointing set of results.

History was a subject I thought I had a good chance of passing, albeit with a low grade, so I decided, as

I progressed through the syllabus, to make some revision notes. Unfortunately, my enthusiasm only lasted for a short time, and subsequent notes were somewhat sparse, only covering the period from the Norman Conquest, in 1066, to the Magna Carta, in 1215. In the exam I was able to answer the first two questions due to my revision notes on this period, but did not have much of a clue about the other six questions; hence, I failed the exam. Maths was a subject that was not bad for me, and Mr Buckley thought I was capable of passing the exam. I was okay at arithmetic but relatively weak at trigonometry and geometry—a dangerous combination for someone wanting to pass the exam. As it turned out I just scraped through with a Grade 6, the lowest pass grade, and, in fact, my only GCE pass.

As the end of my school life loomed, two school friends and I started to plan a holiday for the end of the school year. Money was not in great supply, so it had to be cheap and in the UK, and it was decided that we would go youth hostelling in Devon and Cornwall. The other boys were Richard Other, who had definitely passed more GCEs than me, and Peter Gray. Peter was an interesting person, in that he had never been in the top AA class throughout his time at Hollin, but had decided to go into the fifth year. I suspect this decision was made for him by his wealthy parents who lived in a very nice house near the White Hart Pub in Bowlee, an area between Heywood and Middleton. In order to get down to the West Country, we had to travel by coach, and so in the early days of August we set off on our two-week holiday on a Yelloway coach.

Our first destination was Plymouth, in Devon, and after a long journey of several hours we arrived at the local bus station and then made our way to our first overnight accommodation. I had never before stayed at a youth hostel, so was not sure what to expect, and was pleasantly surprised to find the place welcoming and friendly. The cost of staying at the hostel was cheap, and included an evening meal and breakfast, although you were expected to help prepare the meals and then wash the dishes, etc. after the meal.

So after a fitful night's sleep in a room with several other people exhibiting varying degrees of 'snoring abilities', we set off on our adventure. We had organised our journey in advance, and each day we planned to travel to a specific destination where we knew there was a youth hostel. The plan was to walk together as much as possible and when necessary hitch a lift to our daily destination. It was only later in the holiday that we split up, as hitching a lift for three boys was not that easy.

It is difficult to remember after all these years exactly the route our holiday took, but there were places that have stayed in my mind. Our first destination was Lostwithiel, and the only reason I remember this small town was that within 12 months of starting work at the CWS in Manchester, I was in daily contact with the CWS woollen mill in Lostwithiel, organising the export of their woollen rolls to many different places. One of the places we exported to was Bielefeld, in what was then West Germany, and many years later one of my neighbours originated from Bielefeld, his name being

Peter Klapper. He never did understand the phrase 'running like the clappers'.

We then made our way to St Austell, which did not make much of an impression on me, before crossing into Cornwall and duly arriving in Falmouth, where we stayed for a couple of days. Falmouth was a pleasant place, and in particular I remember the palm trees, something which we definitely did not have in Middleton. From Falmouth we then progressed towards Helston, en route to Penzance, staying in a hostel in Porthleven, a few miles from Helston.

The weather was as you would expect from a British summer, being somewhat mixed, with some hot and some very wet. I am not sure which I preferred, in that the hot days sometimes left us very thirsty, and with the small shops on our route not always having refrigerators for soft drinks, my supposedly refreshing bottle of Ben Shaw's was just a little hot. Also, there was a distinct lack of sun cream in my rucksack; talk about 'mad dogs and Englishmen'. The wet days left us somewhat miserable as we trudged wearily to our next destination, with not many people willing to give us a lift.

Penzance saw us close to the south-west tip of England, and Land's End. In the 1960s Land's End was nothing to write home about, as it was merely a headland approached via a simple pathway, with a sign to signify you were at the very tip of England. A short distance away was the small town of St Just, from where we joined the scenic coast road to St Ives.

During the holiday, communication with home was almost non-existent, the only way being via a public phone box, but we did not have a phone at home. If I remember correctly, I sent my mother several postcards to let her know I was okay.

St Ives was and is one of the most beautiful places in the UK, and in the 1960s was still relatively unspoilt by tourism. I particularly remember the youth hostel, which was in a beautiful location and was definitely a cut above the general standards of these establishments.

We then made our way to Redruth, which then allowed us to be within striking distance of Newquay, a small town on the coast which was rapidly becoming very popular with the younger generation. Surfing, which was then being introduced to Newquay by Australians in the early 1960s, was a major factor in its rise to fame on a global level, taking advantage of the growth of beach culture on the back of the popularity of The Beach Boys.

On leaving Newquay we then started on the road back to Plymouth, and ultimately our journey home. Our last port of call was Liskeard, about 20 miles from Plymouth; but on the morning of our departure from Liskeard there was torrential rain, which threatened to make the final leg of our adventure a miserable experience. We decided to split up, as the chance of a getting a lift was greater while on our own. The first few miles were miserable, and I very quickly became completely wet through; so it was with some relief when someone stopped to give me a lift to Plymouth. It was a lady with a young child, who was on her way to Plymouth to meet her husband who was in the Royal Navy and returning to port on that day. She did say to me that normally she would not pick up hitch-hikers, but in view of the inclement weather and my dishevelled state, she took pity on me, thank God. The weather improved as we got closer to Plymouth, and I arrived in a much drier state, giving my thanks to the lady before making my way to the youth hostel. My two friends duly arrived somewhat later, having eventually managed to obtain a lift.

I mentioned earlier that the youth hostels were friendly and safe places to stay at, but on that evening we encountered someone who was a rather nasty character. I am not entirely sure of how the incident developed, possibly something to do with the small jobs that you had to do while at the hostel. The person was older than us, and when he threatened to beat us up, we spent a very nervous night at the hostel. Fortunately, nothing happened, and we were relieved on the following morning to see him leave the hostel, as we had booked another night before our return home.

While at the hostel we had met two girls, and it was agreed that we would meet them in Plymouth later that day. When we met them, it became clear that I was the odd person out in this situation, and when we later went to the cinema to see *Lawrence of Arabia*, both Richard and Peter quickly sat with the girls, leaving me to find a seat several rows away from them. *C'est la vie.*

So the following morning we boarded the Yelloway coach for our journey back to the North of England, and a few short weeks later, to my final encounter with the ladies from the Pandora pickle factory.